A Teacher's Guide to Support Services

A Teacher's Guide to Support Services

Edited by John Dwyfor Davies
and Pat Davies

NFER-NELSON

Published by The NFER-NELSON Publishing Company Ltd.,
Darville House, 2 Oxford Road East,
Windsor, Berkshire SL4 1DF, England.

First Published 1989

British Library Cataloguing in Publication Data
A Teacher's guide to support services.
   1. Great Britain. Schools. Students with special
   educational needs. Education
   I. Davies, John Dwyfor II. Davies, Pat
   371.9'0941
   ISBN 0-7005-1223-3

Printed in Great Britain by
Billing & Sons Ltd, Worcester

ISBN 0 7005 1223 3
Code 8319 02 4

Contents

Acknowledgements

The editors would like to thank the contributors to this volume for their willingness to cooperate in preparing individual chapters and subsequently responding to numerous requests to modify their texts – often at short notice.

We would also like to take this opportunity to thank Ian Florance and Diana Hilton-Jones for their patient guidance and encouragement whilst the book was in the process of being prepared.

Finally, our thanks to Huw, Gareth and Glyn, for putting up with our preoccupation with this task over an extended period. Their understanding and help has been invaluable.

List of Tables and Figures

List of Contributors

Hazel Bines is a Senior Lecturer in Education at Oxford Polytechnic, whose particular interest is in the area of special educational needs. She has taught in middle and comprehensive schools. She is an active member of the National Association for Remedial Education and the National Council for Special Education. In addition to publishing many articles in educational journals and books, she has also published *Redefining Remedial Education* (Croom Helm, 1986).

Gill Burnham has been working in the home with pre-school children with special needs, since 1975. Her introduction to home intervention was with the Portage project in Cardiff with Roger Blundon in 1976. Since then she has become Head of Service for Home Intervention Programmes in Oxfordshire, where Portage, Makaton and Derbyshire are the main programmes implemented.

Jim Conway is General Adviser (Individual Needs and Evaluation) for Barnsley Local Education Authority. Previously, he was an Adviser for Special needs in Oxfordshire and has also taught in comprehensive and special schools. Recently, he has been concerned with curriculum and staff development, to meet the widening range of educational needs in mainstream schools and colleges. He has published a number of articles on support arrangements in secondary schools and local education authority policy development.

John Dwyfor Davies has experience working in mainstream and special schools. He has worked as a Senior Lecturer at Oxford Polytechnic, where his main contribution was in supporting a range of courses for teachers on special educational needs. Currently he is a Principal Lecturer at Bristol Polytechnic where he is Head of the Special Needs Section in the Department of Education. He has published articles on many topics concerning the education of children with special educational needs, both in the UK and abroad.

Pat Davies has worked for several years in both primary and special schools for children with emotional and behavioural problems, as well as learning difficulties. She is currently a Special Needs

Advisory and Support Teacher in Oxfordshire. She has published widely in educational journals and books, on themes relating to children with learning and behavioural difficulties. She has a particular interest in the areas of early learning and parental involvement in education.

Neville Jones is Principal Educational Psychologist for Oxfordshire. He has written widely on aspects of management and services for pupils with special educational needs, with particular reference to pupils with behavioural difficulties. Between 1969 and 1979, he was Editor of the *Journal of Therapeutic Education*. He has been a member of the Council and Executive Committee of the National Children's Bureau, member of the Executive Committee of the National Association for Mental Health and member of the Consultative Committee on the Schools' Council project on Disturbed Pupils and Gifted Pupils. He coedited *Teacher Training and Special Educational Needs* (1985), *Management of Special Needs: Pupils 11 to 16* (1988) and *Management and the Psychology of Schooling* (1988), and edited *Special Educational Needs Review, No.1* (1988).

John Moore is Senior County Inspector for Special Educational Needs, Kent County Council. He previously held posts in primary, secondary and special schools and was a Senior Lecturer at Oxford Polytechnic from 1979 to 1984. He has co-authored *Someone Else's Problem? Teacher Development to Meet Special Educational Needs* (Falmer Press, 1988) and is the author of 'Perspectives of an LEA officer' in *Lessons in Partnership*, Bedford Way Papers, No.31, 1987. and articles in *Special Children*.

Sarah Sandow is a Principal Lecturer in Special Education at the West London Institute of Higher Education, where she is mainly concerned with in-service education for teachers. She is the co-author of *An Agreed Understanding?* (NFER-NELSON, 1987) in which she explores parent-professional communication with reference to the 1981 Education Act.

Gary Thomas has worked as a teacher, an educational psychologist, and a lecturer in special education. Recently he was Staff Tutor to two School Psychological Services and an Honorary Research Fellow in the Department of Psychology at University College,

London. He is presently a Senior Lecturer at Oxford Polytechnic, School of Education, where he lectures on special educational needs.

Howard Williams is a Senior Psychiatric Social Worker in the Oxfordshire Education Department. He trained as a mathematician and gained qualified teacher status before working as a social worker and Case Work Fellow at the Institute of Marital Studies at the Tavistock Clinic, London. For six years, he was a Senior Lecturer at Oxford Polytechnic, teaching on the Professional Social Work course. He was previously an Area Director in a Social Services Department as well as a Social Work Adviser at the Welsh Office. Since 1975, he has worked in Family and Child Guidance, specializing in Family Therapy.

Julie Wagge is the Deputy District Speech Therapist for the East Berkshire Health Authority and Chief Speech Therapist for the Maidenhead Community. She has worked mainly with children with language disorders in infant, junior and middle school language units in Stevanage, Oxford and Maidenhead. She is a member of the College of Speech Therapists.

Chapter 1
Support in a Changing Context

John Dwyfor Davies and Pat Davies

Over the past decade, debate has highlighted numerous issues central to public perception of the rights of children with special educational needs. The Warnock Report (Warnock, 1978) set out a new conceptual framework for special education, but the issue of integration has remained complex and contentious due to blurred and often confused messages emanating from muted policy and lack of resources.

However, there has been a powerful professional response to the challenges set out in the Warnock Report – despite the practical and organizational nightmare for children, parents and teachers that often accompanies the assessment procedures. The teaching profession has needed to come to terms with a host of organizational, curricular changes, accompanied by philosophical shifts of emphasis.

The rate of change in both primary and secondary education has recently been immense. In the last decade, curriculum development projects have abounded, with new approaches to childrens' reading, writing, numeracy, science and computer technology. Teachers within the secondary sector have had to develop new skills and courses in response to the national initiatives funded by central government. It is now expected that teachers will forge firmer and more open links with industry and commerce. These initiatives and developments have involved teachers in reflecting on wider implications of their role as professional educators.

In addition, the recent devolution of INSET funding arrangements has in many cases resulted in the bombarding of teachers with a rash of courses hurriedly planned and delivered. Attendance at these courses has prompted further questioning of established ideas and practice.

Further changes are now about to be imposed on the profession. The National Curriculum with its assessment procedures and emphasis on competitive proficiency does not marry readily with the positive philosophy of support and integration encompassed in the Warnock Report. Teacher morale is essential to the functioning of a strong support service and to the continuing exploration of how *all* children learn most effectively in our schools.

The Concept of Support

The concept of 'support' is fundamental to the practice and process of integrating children with special educational needs in mainstream schools. The Fish Report (Fish, 1985b) makes the point that if children with special needs are to be offered equal access to the same range of opportunities as their peers, then priority must be given to the development of services that can adequately support individuals and families alike.

Research in this field suggests that local education authorities are presently increasing the number of support personnel available to work with children with special needs (Goacher *et al*, 1987). This confirms the view that the concept of support is becoming increasingly accepted and is growing in popularity. Bowers (1987) adds further weight to this: 'support for the ordinary teacher, whether in the form of an internal specialist or an external-based or "itinerant" colleague, is a model which has proliferated and is likely to go on doing so in the near future'.

The notion of 'support' has mushroomed so quickly that little consensus seems to exist as to its precise nature. It elicits a wide range of meanings within the teaching profession. Hart (1986) states that '...no generally agreed definition of support teaching actually exists'.

Bowers (1987) is one of the few who has attempted to distinguish between major groups currently subsumed by the term. He has drawn a clear distinction between 'internal' or 'external' support and 'consultancy', and discusses the constraints and implications of the two groups of professionals working together for a common end.

Despite the limited research conducted into the viability and value of support models, local education authorities have evolved their own pattern of provision and this tends to reflect the particular philosophy adopted by each authority. Consequently, there tends to be a wide discrepancy between the nature of support available for children with special needs in different authorities (Pearson and Lindsay, 1987). Gipps, Gross and Goldstein (1987) also identify considerable variation between authorities in the number of personnel made available to support children with special educational needs.

A similar discrepancy is found not only in the nature of the support available *between* local education authorities, but also *within* a single authority. This is particularly apparent where a policy of regionalization encourages each region or division to develop its own pattern of support. Children with special educational needs are then likely to receive significantly different forms of support (which may also vary in quality), according to where they happen to live. This is again contrary to the intent of the Warnock Report, which sought to ensure *equality* of provision for children with special educational needs.

Several problems have emerged as a result of the development of an expanding support service. If a support service is to be effective, several key issues will have to be addressed and a cohesive policy adopted by local education authorities. Amongst the major problems confronting the administrators charged with providing such a service, the following seem to be uppermost:

- maximising resources;
- dependency or ownership of responsibility;
- attitudinal change;
- the focus of support;
- collaboration and negotiation.

Maximizing resources

Local education authorities have developed a network of professionals concerned with offering 'support' for children with special needs. These include:
- General advisers
- Special Needs Advisers
- Educational Psychologists
- Clinical Psychologists
- Educational Social Workers

- Psychiatric Social Workers
- Special Needs Advisory and Support Teachers
- Home/school Advisory Teachers
- Pre-school Counsellors

– as well as professional support from health and social services.

Arguably, each professional has a particular range of expertise and skills which can aid the progress of a child with special needs. It is likely, however, that unless the delivery of support is carefully managed, one of two things will result – either duplication of resources, or an uneven pattern of support may occur. Apart from the obvious resource implications, there is an additional likelihood that where coordination is ill-defined, conflicting advice and recommendations may be offered to the recipient, resulting from differing perspectives and professional priorities. This can lead to confusion and conflict amongst all concerned – recipients and supporters alike.

The Warnock Committee (Warnock, 1978) anticipated the dangers in developing a wide range of support agencies and identified the need to coordinate the various agencies concerned in supporting children. In this way, the advantages of support could be maximized.

It would be naïve to suggest that such a coordinating role is free from complications; neither does it provide a universal solution to the difficulties presently experienced by those involved in the supporting task. In Chapter 5, Jim Conway describes some of the major difficulties confronting those involved in establishing a more coordinated approach; he also supports the view that a unified system is likely to be necessary if the expectations and the rights of those concerned are to be realized.

At a time when the education service is becoming increasingly concerned with cost-effectiveness, local authority officers must look closely at the financial implications of the support services offered. One major driving force behind the movement to integrate children with special needs in mainstream schools, has been the argument that this form of provision is economically advantageous because it can reduce the financial commitment to maintaining and running expensive resources for segregated provision. Hegarty and Pocklington (1981) however, have argued that such assumptions are ill-founded and that the support necessary to implement a policy of integration is every bit as costly as the alternatives.

Dependency or ownership of responsibility

It can be argued that where a wide range of support is made available, the very act of providing this support can itself be a disadvantage to the child. The presence of professionals other than the class teacher, acting in a supporting capacity, can cause the child to become dependent upon such support. Dependency may well result in difficulties for the child when that support is withdrawn – through changing patterns of practice, or through the child reaching an age when the authority is no longer obliged to provide for his or her needs.

It can also be argued that the very presence of a support agent may inadvertently draw further attention to the child's difficulties. This well-intentioned intervention can result in other children regarding the child as 'special' or 'different' and labelling him or her as such. This may be a particular danger for those who have secured support for less tangible reasons, and whose needs are not immediately evident to their peers, such as children with learning difficulties.

From the teachers' point of view, the danger of assuming and devolving responsibility to the 'expert' support agent can be equally debilitating. In the first place, it assumes that the others have skills and expertise not possessed by the class teacher and this implies a second-rate professional status. At the same time, it could lead to the abdication of responsibility for the childs' progress and development. If others are seen as 'responsible' for this, then the class teacher may reduce the degree of responsibility necessary for appropriate progress to be achieved.

Attitudinal change

The successful development of a range of support services implies that considerable adaptations would need to be made in traditional attitudes held by the agencies concerned. If one group of professionals adopts in isolation a particular stance regarding a central concept, then the notion of an integrated and cohesive service will not be realized. This is a particularly important factor when the climate surrounding the education of children with special educational needs is rapidly changing. Maggie Balshaw (1987) has pointed out that for the class teacher, the pressure of assuming increased responsibility for the successful education of children with special needs can be a particularly daunting prospect and one that demands a significant shift in fundamental attitudes. The development of the new role suggested for classroom teachers will require clear guidance and assistance. It is futile to assume that all teachers will accept these demands unquestioningly and gladly. Developing a team approach to working with children demands careful planning and sophisticated management.

The problem becomes further compounded when the respective role of a large number of different agencies is involved. The list offered above indicates the range of possible professionals who can be included within the support team. A major difficulty arises concerning the traditional hierarchies seen among professionals. Even within one school the question of responsibility, defined by status, is a potential stumbling block. This is considerably increased when medical, psychological, social and educational representatives are all involved. Professionals from all these services need to continually question their own practices, make informed decisions and communicate sensitively in varied settings. The concepts of ownership and collaboration need to be constantly borne in mind by all professionals involved in decision-making and policy reviews. This will require many professionals to make a considerable shift in attitude and in their individual perceptions of interprofessional support work.

The focus of support

Attention is drawn above to the wide interpretation of the concept of support. A major dilemma confronting those involved in the process of support is the clarification of the direction to which they are targeting their attention and efforts. Dyer (1988) summarizes this dilemma by asking: 'Whom is the support teacher supporting? The child, the teacher, the family or the curriculum?' Resolving these fundamental questions is essential in order to develop a comprehensive and effective service.

The evidence supplied by Gipps and Goldstein (op. cit.) suggests that there is a tendency to focus more directly on support for the class teacher and in particular, a focus on curriculum support. This is not to negate the need for support in the other areas, but identifies a developing priority.

There is at present lively debate within the profession generally as to the advantages accrued by support agencies when they are involved in working across the dimensions identified here. The limitations experienced by those within the support services who have tended to focus on one particular aspect only suggests that a *wider* brief might be more beneficial. Here again, the necessity for close monitoring and management becomes increasingly apparent: the evils of a multiplicity of agencies and role conflict must not to be perpetuated.

Collaboration and negotiation

Opportunities have to be created in which all relevant professionals can jointly explore the implications of any changes in policy relating to provision for children with difficulties. The support teacher needs to encourage an atmosphere of positive professional exchange, through which mutual respect and understanding can be fostered. Through such discussions colleagues may be reminded of, or introduced to, alternative approaches that may often be applicable to other situations. If the professionals can be seen as flexible and willing to work within whatever structure emerges from this dialogue, then the message conveyed is that the support role is dynamic and responsive, diminishing the view that it is prescriptive, with predictable and limited strategies.

Closely related to collaboration is the concept of shared responsibility. This encompasses the notion that even within those environments whose perceptions and boundaries are tightly drawn, input from more than one source may be required. Feeling 'in control' within one's own domain has to be tempered with an openness to hearing the views of others and the acknowledgement of joint responsibility.

Margaret Donaldson (1978) suggests that professional educators should encourage students to come to grips with incongruity and even to seek it out in a positive fashion, enjoying challenge. Equally, they should aim to discourage defence and withdrawal. This implies that a major element of the supportive role should assume a pro-active and dynamic stance, stimulating innovation through reflection and subsequent constructive debate.

A major concern for those involved in supportive roles is the constant tendency to dwell on difficulties resulting from different perceptions and expectations. Yet support teachers who share successful practice with other professionals realize the powerful impact on motivation and are likely to seek further collaboration, which will enhance the experiences offered to children. Margaret Donaldson (1978) noted the need to 'draw a distinction between reward and recognition and to acknowledge how strong a need we have to communicate achievement to our fellow men and to see it confirmed in their eyes.'

Learning to fail

The government decision to introduce a national core curriculum, together with assessment at the ages of seven, 11, 14 and 16 is likely to have major repercussions for all involved in supporting children with special educational needs. Since the implementation of the 1981 Education Act, many of these children (who make up at least 20 per cent of the total school population) have moved out of the separate provision of the special school or special unit, into mainstream classes. Models of provision vary, but the goal remains the same – access to the curriculum for children who in the past might have been excluded from the experiences of their peers.

Underlying the 'bench-mark' approach is the view that normal development follows a clearly-determined pattern. This approach leaves no place for individual difference, or for varying rates of development. The changes in attitude that the 1981 Education Act aimed to bring about might well be undermined by what seems to be a return to a pass/fail approach. In a young child, self-image is strongly influenced by the value other people place upon him and by the opportunities available for meaningful and purposeful learning. The child who enters school and copes with new challenges will be highly valued by his teachers; all too often, the child who initially fails to meet these challenges will not receive such approval. If a child's failure is further confirmed by an inability to perform according to a norm related test at prescribed ages, that child will almost certainly be alienated and withdraw from challenging situations (Donaldson, 1978).

The double-edged sword which cuts through layers of low self-esteem and failure is the respect and value that we, as professionals, have for both children and their parents. This can only develop through an ongoing analysis of both practice and interaction. For those involved in supporting children with learning difficulties, it will become imperative not to lose sight of the prime (though complex) task by being lulled into colluding with the system at the expense of the individual.

As a result of this legislation, many schools will feel pressured to exclude children with learning difficulties so that the profile of the school may remain high in the eyes of the community in general. The publication of success and failure rates at 'bench-mark' stages, is likely to encourage the exclusion of those children experiencing difficulty from 'prime' schools. If this pattern were to become widespread, the implications for supporting agencies would be profound. Support teachers might be seen as second-class professionals, as 'definers of difficulties'.

Classroom teachers fighting for the *exclusion*, rather than the *integration*, of children with special needs, may well be less likely to cooperate with the support services; if the school appears unable to provide appropriate resources to support such children, transfer to a special school will appear as in the best interests of all concerned.

Networking
Widlake (1986) suggests that

meeting the educational needs of disadvantaged pupils requires changes in the traditional roles performed by teachers, social workers, health visitors and others.

Whatever else, the role defined by the term 'professional' should include a capacity for systematic change. Being a professional does not require a rigid adherence to a predetermined role. Indeed, one of the hallmarks of successful professionals has been just this capacity to adapt and redefine their own expertise together with the ability to convince others that their expertise is still genuine, useful and relevant.

It may therefore be desirable for the professionals involved in the support services to be more actively engaged in structuring situations through which increased trust and understanding can be developed. This may include shared responsibility between professions in establishing, leading and running joint in-service sessions, through which issues of mutual concern can be explored and techniques and strategies developed.

Within the field of special education, attitude change is seen as central in in-service training, combined with a whole-school and interprofessional commitment to enhancing the quality of the experiences offered to children with special needs. Where professionals working within a community have identified a common purpose and intent, they are more likely to resolve potential barriers to the development of interprofessional support systems.

This volume attempts to address some of the major issues confronting the support agencies in the late 1980s and into the 1990s. It further attempts to define the major roles executed by key professionals within the support system and to project how these are likely to develop within the forseeable future. The general principle that underpins the book is that children with special educational needs should not be viewed as passive recipients of predetermined knowledge and prescribed programmes delivered by the support agencies. The role of the support agencies is viewed as a collaborative search for the optimum form of provision in which children can discover and develop their individual talents. Individual contributors, however, may adopt a stance which is occasionally at variance with this. The editors acknowledge the diversity in professional opinion and have not attempted to modify this view where it is expressed.

The chapter by Pat Davies (see page 22) sets the scene for support and reflects on emerging trends in the light of practical experience within one district. Jim Conway takes a broader view and having reviewed developing trends through reference to recent surveys, addresses key concepts and dilemmas confronting support workers (see page 49).

John Moore (refer to page 135) discusses the complex task of coordinating and integrating support services, as perceived by a local education inspector who is responsible for refining such a service for one authority. He focusses on the management issues that such a task invariably presents and considers the marrying of a philosophical model to its practical implications.

Sarah Sandow (see page 125) describes the importance of parental involvement within the support process and draws on her recent research within this field in order to comment on parental and professional perspectives and aspirations for such a service.

In 'Broadening the Role of the Support Teacher', John and Pat Davies highlight the important position held by support teachers in achieving effective change with schools. This draws attention away from the traditional role occupied by peripatetic teachers and projects a more pro-active function for such professionals.

Gill Burnham, Hazel Bines, Gary Thomas, Howard Williams and Julie Wagge each present a specialized perspective and consider the challenges facing a range of professionals involved in supporting children with special educational needs.

Gill Burnham describes the development of a pre-school service for supporting young children and their parents. She examines the importance of home-intervention programmes and suggests how these can be made most effective. See page 12.

Hazel Bines (page 36) draws on both her wide experience in secondary schools and her recent research into support for children with special needs in secondary schools. She suggests that a more holistic approach be adopted if secondary schools are to be successful in their attempts to provide an adequate service for children with special educational needs.

Gary Thomas looks at the changing role of the educational psychologist as a support agent (see page 64). Having considered the reasons for the necessity for change, central foci for future developments in the role of the educational psychologist working within schools are suggested.

Howard Williams places the role of the psychiatric social worker in a context which takes account of recent developments within the field. He draws on case studies to illustrate the way in which this role is now progressing, and suggests a need for further collaboration between agencies. His chapter begins on page 76.

Julie Wagge, having described the role of the speech therapist and its place within the range of provision for children with special needs, identifies pathways available to teachers through which fuller and more appropriate use may be made of the speech therapy provision. Refer to page 93.

The final chapter in this book (see page 145) considers the very central role that in-service education holds in the development of provision for children with special educational needs. Neville Jones examines the needs and styles of in-service education for the provision of support in the next decade.

Chapter 2
Supporting Families and Educating Children with Special Needs in the Early Years

Gill Burnham

1971 was an important milestone in the history of special education in this county, for it was at that time all children were deemed
to be educable. Prior to that date, children who were seen as mentally handicapped were considered to be outside the education system and were the responsibility of the health authorities. In 1973
The Berkshire Education Authority, and some other local education authorities, introduced the concept of early support to the parents of mentally handicapped pre-school children in the form of
the Pre-School Teacher Counselling Service. They were pioneers
in working with, and supporting, parents as the first educators of
their children. In 1974, as a result of the change in county boundaries, Oxfordshire carried on the services of the pre-school counselling service. Pre-School counsellors at that time discussed with
parents the day-to-day management of their child and parental
expectation in the context of the child's handicapping condition.
Advice and support was often demonstrated through play activities, but the process lacked structure and direction. Within five
years of the education authorities taking over responsibility for these
children, the government set up an inquiry into the education of
all children with handicapping conditions and the result of this was
the Warnock Report.

The Warnock Report (Warnock, 1978) has had considerable
influence on the educational experience offered to children under
the age of five. The Report could be likened to a great wave which
brought with it many new educational ideas and concepts. We have

now entered into a far calmer period of consolidation and evaluation. The Warnock Committee recognized difficulties in trying to fit children into defined categories, when many had difficulties in more than one area. There was an obvious need for a more meaningful description of each child as an individual. This involved the notion of a multiprofessional assessment. Thus, the global terminology of 'children with special needs' indicated that there was concern for a fuller description of the child's needs. This resulted in professionals acknowledging the existence of a broader spectrum of children with special educational needs. It also enabled children to move in an out of specialized provision according to their needs. In practice, this increased the importance of pre-school checks done by health visitors, (usually at eight months, 18 months, three years and five years). These checks often alerted professionals to difficulties being experienced by very young children and resulted in support being offered to families within their own home.

The second 'wave' following Warnock was the introduction of the concept of integration. The notion of mainstream integration and the abolition of distinct categories of handicaps gave pre-school professionals grounds for much counselling work with parents. Parental fears and anxieties need to be shared and their experiences measured against local provision.

Successful integration depends upon a desire and ability of the host school, nursery or playgroup to give the child the most suitable pre-school experience. Thus the home teacher needs to be able to communicate and work within a multidisciplinary setting. He or she should, if this has not already been arranged, draw together psychologists, educationalists, medical and paramedical services, and parents: this will often be facilitated through the use of an assessment centre. The 1981 Education Act makes provision for integration of this kind. However, parental support during this process may be provided by whichever professional has already established a link with parents: usually this is the home teacher, who may by now have become a 'friend' of the family.

The third 'wave' which has had a great influence on the pre-school child, is the sharing of the Portage home intervention model which started in this country in the Wessex region and Gwent (Bluma *et al.*, 1987). The pioneer work with this American model by the Wessex team was used in evidence for the Warnock Report and influenced greatly the recommendations that were made. In 1969, the United States provided centrally-funded money for each State to originate programmes under the title of 'Handicapped children's early education projects' and to this day there are a variety of parental intervention progammes running throughout each State. The Portage model bases its philosophy on using parents as the educators of their children. This involves weekly home visits for one hour to each home, giving parents clear educational goals to be achieved.

The parent is left with a clear criteria, how to teach towards the goal, and how to reward the child. The programme is commercially available in a form that includes developmental skills and ideas on how each skill may be taught. The package is so structured as to allow professionals from any discipline to work with the families. Volunteers can also work in the families, as long as there is back-up support structure, including regular supervision.

In 1986, the British government introduced a support grant to local authorities to enable them to set up pre-school services meeting the general criteria of the Portage Model. This enabled a considerable expansion of services for the pre-school special needs child. The groups of professionals using the Portage criteria in the United Kingdom include health visitors, social workers, psychologists, teachers and volunteers under the guidance of professionals. The main characteristics of the Portage home-based early intervention model (Bluma, Shearer *et al.*, 1987), are:

- The educational programme takes place in each child's home and is implemented by a home teacher who visits each family weekly.
- Assessment procedures inventory the child's competences as a basis for preparing an individualised curriculum.
- Teaching methods are based on applied behaviour analysis.
- Curriculum is planned with the expectation that the child will achieve the prescribed short term goals within a week.
- Parents work with their child during the week: they are in fact the child's teacher.
- Weekly staff meetings are held to solve problems as a team and to modiify curriculum.

The home teaching service provides a number of advantages. First, it offers parents a course of action that is positive and helpful to their child. Secondly, it requires parents to form a relationship with a regular visitor to their home. When a family first learns that their child has a special need, (whether this is at birth or later in the child's life) the effect is traumatic. The emotions felt have often been equated with grief – the child they thought they had is lost and replaced with one who now differs from their expectations. It is recognized that some of the emotions associated with grief include guilt, anger, blame and remorse; and there is a need to work through these feelings by 'doing'. Following a bereavement, preparing for the funeral, dealing with personal papers and talking with and supporting other members of the family all help the bereaved come to terms with their loss.

The feeling of guilt among families of special needs children is, 'What have I done to bring this onto my child, my family and myself?' This and many other such questions are addressed to psychologists and paediatricians and repeated to other professionals in the home, such as health visitors, social workers and therapists. The feeling of anger prompts questions like 'Who caused this to happen?' or 'Who is at fault, and *where* and *when* did things go wrong?' and is often directed at the person bringing the news and how, when or where the unwanted information was imparted. Further anger is engendered if questions are not answered or if the answers are misunderstood. Thus it is helpful for parents to see the professional (usually a paediatrician) frequently during the first few weeks. The misunderstanding of information when 'in shock' is common. It is important at this time to encourage the family to talk extensively about its feelings and anxieties. There follows the need to *do* something. Families can initially busy themselves gathering relevant information. This, however, can often leave them still more bewildered and afraid of the future. Occasionally parents may turn to a local organization, although in general this rarely happens at first, as groups of people can be overwhelming as well as comforting. It is not unusual for parents to come to a group situation about six months or a year after first being told. Groups are often particularly useful to parents experiencing the trauma with an older child following illness or an accident.

The need for 'activity' may be addressed by structured teaching programmes which aim to help the members of a family to work together in making the most of their child's potential. Involvement in such programmes may also compensate a little for the feelings of guilt that are part of the 'grieving' process. Grieving can recur whenever new information is given or a new dimension of the child's condition emerges. When looking at their child's first needs for schooling, for example, anger and 'high activity' are often seen in parents. Support at this time is important. Parents' needs to express their feelings and opinions should be recognized; they should also be encouraged to question the views of *professionals* involved, but sometimes *their own* attitudes as well.

They need to consider the child's needs as well as their own. All too often professionals seeing a family once or twice can label them as 'uncooperative' and 'difficult', whereas with time to discuss with other professionals or parents in a similar position, more balanced decisions and judgements can be made.

The media often highlight successful intervention with specific individuals. Thus the guilt parents may feel is fuelled if they choose not to follow (for example) a programme involving eight hours a day intensive therapy, assisted by an army of helpers. For them, other considerations such as expense, total family commitment, may have to be taken into consideration; yet they may be left wondering what might have happened had they decided to take a different course of action. Likewise, other families travel across continents to secure treatment which they believe will help their child. For some it works but for others it may not.

The Portage programme requires a commitment of time. This has to be negotiated between the home visitor and the parents, and will range from five minutes a day to several periods of 15 minutes a day. Even though the commitment required is relatively small, parents do not always comply. What we have to address is why, and does such 'cheating' *matter*, or does it merely feed parents' feelings of guilt? Parents who need to be active will draw in many professionals and will then, according to their own needs, try to follow all the advice or programmes suggested. For some families, this will mean organizing large numbers of people to help them in the programme for their particular child.

Programmed Learning

Programmed learning exists on a continuum of time: this may range from a specific five minutes a day, when a child will be taught a specific skill; to four hours a day being set aside for prescribed exercises and a routine of set activities; to eight hours a day of exercise patterning and routine rote learning. The one fact that will be constant is that the child is in a structured situation, working one-to-one with an adult. An awareness of the child's natural play level, is essential if his or her innate motivation is to be harnessed: no child should be taught 'tricks' in isolation.

Children used to be prepared for the 11+ exams in order to answer a paper correctly: we may now be in danger of doing something similar with programmed learning, teaching children how to execute checklists of tasks. Alongside the programmes it is important to *consolidate* learning for the child so that he or she can use a newly-acquired skill in a wide variety of ways, learning from failure as well as success. In Oxfordshire a range of programmes are used including *The Portage Early Education Programme* (Bluma *et al.*, 1987), Parent Involvement charts from the Hester Adrian Foundation, the *Derbyshire Language Scheme* (Knowles and Masidlover, 1982) Makaton language programme, Roy McConkey's play programme, the *SKI*HI* (*Sensory Impaired, Hearing Impaired*) home intervention programme for hearing-impaired children, Esther Cotton's work on Basic Motor Pattern; the work of Dr. Geoffrey Waldon is also being looked at for future possible use. Just as the teacher in the classroom may offer a range of reading opportunities, so may the Home Teacher develop appropriate teaching strategies and programmes for the special needs child before the age of five; plus choosing from a range of published programmes.

Portage offers a structured checklist and a behaviour modification approach when required. PIP charts from the Hester Adrian Foundation similarly check the skills a child has, but this scheme is not as specific in how to teach. Roy McConkey's work since leaving the Hester Adrian Foundation has focused on skills to be taught in a general situation, encouraging parents and teachers to *teach* and then *observe* the child's use of the skills. The Derbyshire Language model helps people working in the home to share with the parents the analysis of language – the comprehension level as well as the expressive levels achieved. The pre-school teacher needs to emphasize that communication may be eased when a child understands non-verbal clues.

The need to aid language with gesture in some children can be enhanced by the use of Makaton sign language. The project with pre-school Down's Syndrome children in Oxfordshire, where Makaton was used with children as young as six months old, has shown the value of early intervention. The system encourages the use of speech, facial expression and structured gesture in order to form a communication picture. The child is able to use gesture alongside early attempts at speech, thus giving the parents a clearer understanding of what he or she is trying to communicate. Their response will encourage the child, whereas previous attempts at communication may have been so frustrating that they served only to discourage the child from continuing his attempts at communicating.

The work of Esther Cotton looking at the 'Basic Motor Pattern' of the cerebral palsy child gives us further awareness of movement (including function) in a child's activities. The positioning, timing and breakdown of the movements a child with motor disorder can initiate for him or herself adds to the methods employed. Sharing with parents their child's individual needs, as well as the parents' needs when working with their child, is an important part of the pre-school teachers' role.

The work of Dr. Geoffrey Waldon, mainly with autistic children and their families, helps us look at the 'social' pressure we place on the child's activity; in general, children are able to learn through frequent repetition executed in a variety of ways, using space and gross movement. Geoffrey Waldon suggests that the handicapping behaviour of children with special needs is to some extent created by the environment and society; this concept helps the parent and teacher work alongside the child in a more sensitive, thoughtful and structured way, providing him or her with secure boundaries.

The final programme mentioned is *SKI*HI (Sensory Impaired, Hearing Impaired)*, which was developed in Utah, USA by Dr. Tom Clark in 1972. This is a home intervention model for hearing-impaired children, and identifies four main areas of concern for the parents of the hearing-impaired child:

- hearing aid management;
- auditory awareness skills;
- communication skills;
- language skills.

The programme supports the parents within each of these areas with activities designed to focus on the skill being taught using the following four areas of the child's daily life:

- play;

- self-care;
- helping with household chores;
- out of doors.

Parents need no longer feel bound to set aside time to 'teach'; instead they become increasingly aware of all the opportunities offered to reinforce particular areas of learning. The different programmes available give the professionals choice in how to share with parents appropriate responses to the needs of their child; they will thus help parents to expand the special expertise they already have with their child.

Frequency of visits

The Portage model emphasizes the importance of a weekly visit. This is necessary when parents have been given a very structured programme to follow between visits, the model always remaining that of 'parent educator'. The pursuance of goals needs to be negotiated clearly, parental expectations clearly stated and the home-teacher's contribution to this project specified.

It is my experience that the home-teacher's role in enabling parents to observe their childs' development, noting and monitoring small behavioural changes generally takes about 18 months to two years. Frequent visits are necessary during this time, since families may need encouragement with fresh ideas about play and home-based learning activities. The home visitor focuses on the child during this phase. More generalized activities become central to the child's growth and development.

During this period, the pre-school nursery or playgroup experience will need to be encouraged or arranged. When starting any form of pre-school provision, the home-visitor takes on the role of coordinator between home and school, supporting parents whose child has special educational needs, in this new experience of facing the 'systems' outside their home. For home intervention programmes to continue, we must ensure that:

- the programmes we follow do not lead us into the old trap of 'labelling' children according to medical diagnoses;
- after a home visit the home teacher always asks questions like

'What feelings have I left these parents with? What activity have I left for them to carry out? Was my visit meaningful and worthwhile?'

- the programme is suited to the individual family's need and is not intrusive upon the family;

- the professional development of personnel working with the pre-school child ensures that the pre-school teacher is unblinkered and constantly aware of the exciting initiatives being made in the UK, as well as in other parts of the world. These initiatives may well be occurring outside the home-teacher's own sphere; multidisciplinary communication and inservice training is therefore vital.

- local education authorities prepare themseves to maintain recently-developed services after the end of the government-funding arrangements in 1989.

The benefits of home visiting are not always derived from the frequency of visits but rather from the support and encouragement which parents receive as a result.

Conclusion

It is recognized that parents are the first educators of their children. The Warnock Report encouraged the government to support the thinking that the need for a home intervention model (for the child under five and his or her family) is best met through the Portage project model, which has been well-researched and packaged: a wealth of Portage material is available. The 'behaviour modification' approach when working with young children who have special needs is useful, but is not sufficient alone. The individual needs of *parents*, as well those of the *child* should be a strong guide when choosing how best to interact. In fact it may be that styles of education change as the needs of the child and family change. The overriding constraint is the parents' awareness of the child's development and how this development can be broken down into small, manageable steps. The reward systems may be highly-structured or may be inherent in the activity. The parent and professionals can share in the process of observation and by the extent to which the child uses a new skill will be able to ascertain whether it has been genuinely acquired (and is thus transferable to other areas of his or her daily life) or is simply a 'trick'.

To support parents through these new areas of awareness, the person working in the home needs to be aware of stages in the 'grieving' process and how these relate to the parents' needs and attitudes; the professional also needs to be aware that some of the symptoms of grief may re-emerge as new and significant information is imparted. Working with families in this way is both rewarding and stressful, but above all it requires a high level of sensitivity and professionalism.

Chapter 3
Consultancy and Support – an Overview of Present Practice

Pat Davies

The 1980s have witnessed a marked shift in the perception of educationalists regarding the rights of those children who require support in the mainstream school. The Warnock Report (Warnock, 1978) and the 1981 Education Act, followed by the Fish Report (Fish, 1985), gave philosophical backing for an end to segregated provision for young people with special needs.

> Equal access to, and participation in, society demands respect for children and young people with disabilities and their families. Wherever they are educated, work and enjoy their leisure, these children and young people, like all others whatever their race, class and gender, must be acknowledged with current and potential abilities to contribute to society. (Fish Report 1985)

The underlying intent of both legislation and Reports has been inspirational, as is evident in the diverse range of opportunities offered to many of our exceptional children in playgroups, nursery classes and primary schools throughout the country. Welton and Evans (1985) state that The Policy and Provision for Special Needs Project Team found that despite difficulties caused by lack of resources, there was a positive response to the philosophy behind the Act. There was, for example, a great concern to involve parents in assessment procedures and to give them adequate information. There was also more willingness to consider the placement of children with special needs in mainstream schools and to provide more innovative ways of offering support.

Parallel to this shift in emphasis, the movement towards more active participation by parents in the education of their young children has made a powerful impact. The educational justification for such partnership stems largely from the extensive research evidence examining those variables which measure the ability of young children to learn most effectively (Widlake, 1986; Wells, 1984; Tizard and Hughes, 1984).

The potency of parents as joint educators has been increasingly acknowledged in many of our schools. This trend has been further influenced by evidence that stresses the positive short- and long-term effects of parental involvement in the early education of their children. Many professionals, as well as parents, have (either directly or indirectly) been part of the British version of a 'Headstart'-type programme – the voluntary community playgroup. Through this involvement, they have not only gained greater understanding of how young children learn, but have also become aware of the significance of their own contribution to this process. At the same time, the cumulative evidence of the powerful effect of parental support in developing young childrens' literacy and language skills has influenced professional perception and practice in encouraging the notion of parents as equal educators of their children.

One of the major ways by which many local authorities have encompassed both notions (integration *and* parental participation) is by establishing a new strain of professional – the consultant support teacher. The precise role of the consultant support teacher varies from authority to authority and even within a single authority, reflecting local responses to perceived needs. Nevertheless, one of the main functions of the support teacher is to encourage head- and class-teachers to consider ways of maximizing learning opportunities for children with special needs in ordinary schools. Their perception of the support, as being either teacher-focused or child-focused, will ultimately affect the way this support is offered.

The Exploratory Nature of the Role

Legislation alone will not achieve effective change in the educational system. Change is dependent upon the complex interplay of attitudes held by those who are involved in such a dynamic social process. Welton and Evans (1986) suggests that adaptions of behaviour and relationships may or may not be the intended outcome of the policies and guidelines issued by local authorities or 'reflections of the policy intentions of the government, which sought to shape structures and behaviour through legislation'. Weatherley (1979) contends that the behaviour of 'street-level bureaucrats' is highly discretionary and maintains that *individuals*, rather than organizations, construct policy to enable them to survive and to continue to deliver to their clients such a service as they are able in a new and changing situation. This adaptive behaviour is intended to be an appropriate response to local circumstances and a creative development which will eventually lead to a wider change in consensus about the policy intention.

As a result of the wide and ambiguous role that support teachers are presented with, individuals interpret the role in such a way as to reflect their own professional philosophy. Consequently, emphasis will vary *within* teams as well as *between* them, reflecting the wide spectrum of what is understood by 'special educational need' and by what constitutes an effective support model.

Dispelling Myths

Support teachers are also caught up in the uncertain boundaries and responsibilities regarding children with special needs; these uncertainties stem from confused assumptions as to the location of special needs within the individual child. Paradoxically, the 1981 Education Act reinforced this confusion by its focus on the assessment and statementing procedures and their accompanying notions of 'handicap' and specialist jargon.

The continued existence of specialist provision and separate advisory services hampers and frustrates the progress of innovative integration. The challenge for both head teachers and support staff is to create a balance between focusing on the *context* in which the child experiences difficulties in learning (and thus on a whole-curriculum, inclusive approach) and taking the risk that those children with particular needs may slip through the net in the name of *integration*.

The greatest challenge with which support teachers are presented is to develop ways of resolving and managing problems with the full cooperation of all parties involved and, by so doing, to dispel the myths surrounding the intrusion of the external 'expert'. Paul Widlake (1986) suggests that the hallmark of true professionals, whatever their discipline, is the ability to adapt and redefine their own expertise and to be able to convince others that their expertise is genuine and useful. In many instances, meeting this challenge is facilitated by a strong sense of professionalism, which covers all their dealings with children with special needs. Numerous 'ordinary' class teachers are positive and quietly confident as a result of working successfully with children with learning difficulties. Paternalistic notions of benevolence and tolerance have been replaced by respect and a determination to maximize the potential of each child. As the class teacher is the key person in influencing opportunities on offer, it is essential for the support teacher to recognize the communality of skills and to establish a shared purpose.

The Support Teacher's Changing Role: A Case Study

Background

In 1983/84, many primary head teachers in East Oxfordshire voiced concern regarding the implementation of the Warnock Report and the 1981 Education Act in times of financial constraint. Also, many head teachers had expressed doubts about the efficacy of traditional remedial practices and the concept of peripatetic teachers working with children on a withdrawal basis. In response, a team of teachers was established in East Oxfordshire in September 1984, to support children with learning difficulties in cooperation with other helping agencies. It was concerned with offering support through direct teaching as well as supporting class teachers and parents. Discussions with local education authority officers and advisory staff led to a joint reappraisal of existing provision and ways of widening the concept of support to encompass not only the child, but also all those integral to his wider educational experiences – teachers, parents, peers and other professionals.

The scope of the work was defined as follows:

- Advising heads, teachers and parents on methods and materials for particular children with learning difficulties.

- Spending a regular amount of time teaching chidren with serious learning difficulties, or working with other children to enable the class teacher to focus on the children with difficulties.

- Helping teachers set up and develop suitable resources and learning materials.

- Cooperation in the provision of relevant in-service training and in the professional development of teachers.

- Cooperation with colleagues in the support services who may include pre-school counsellors, educational psychologists, social workers, health visitors, and so on.

- Liaison with the appropriate secondary schools.

The formation of a resource centre as a focal point for all the helping agencies, both statutory and voluntary, as well as for heads, class teachers and parents proved invaluable.

Within the centre, ideas, suggestions and approaches have been explored in a welcoming atmosphere and where books and materials could be reviewed or made. It also provided a base in which team members could reflect and continuously reassess assumptions on which their practice was based. It also provided a centre for in-service courses or informal discussions with school staffs.

Changing considerations

Team members shared common aims which had evolved through previous experience and through discussion in individual schools and with members of the management group (consisting of head teachers, advisers and educational psychologists). Many fundamental issues raised within these discussions were disconcerting, not least to the support team. These encompassed such issues as:

- remediation versus the holistic approach;
- skills-based approach versus the child-centred approach;
- within-child versus within-the-curriculum;

- withdrawal versus classroom-based work;
- objectives versus an eclectic approach;
- behavioural versus counselling;
- learnt helplessness versus confidence.

Traditionally, teachers has sought solutions which relinquished to support teachers the responsibility for the teaching of pupils with learning difficulties. Alternatively, they may have required the support teacher to *diagnose* the source of learning problems, *itemize* the deficiencies and *prescribe* the correct dose of activities to be undertaken (or materials to be used) which would enable the child to 'get better' and therefore to catch up in basic skills areas. It is easy to understand why many support agencies adopted a model of practice that would collude with this view.

However, several questions re-emerged:

- What value was such support to the recipients?

- Did the new role differ from that of the *traditional* peripatetic remedial service, and was it more effective?

- Were the support teachers continuing to transmit the same messages – that the problems were located within the children and that only outside 'experts' could diagnose and identify what might be helpful for the referred child?

Emerging directions

As a result of the interchange of ideas outlined above, and an analysis of practice within schools, the following aims emerged:

- To present support as a dynamic response to the needs of children, recognizing differing patterns of development and motivation.

- To enable head teachers and teachers to develop their perception of the role of support teachers, moving away from the notion of prop or crutch, to that of a facilitator.

- To maximize peer group support.

- To increase the awareness of appropriate interaction between adults and children in the classroom and in the home.

- To support initiatives designed to encourage parental interest and responsibility in the education of their children.

- To encourage all concerned to appreciate the interdependence of the range of personnel in meeting the educational needs of children. This should help to relieve the anxieties that individuals may otherwise experience as a result of a child's failure to learn a range of complex skills.

It was also realized that support teachers need to be clear about their objectives and to agree with school staff on the basis of support and collaboration. Decisions on the form of intervention, and how it is to be monitored and evaluated, also need to be discussed and mutually agreed. Through such discussion, central issues about responsibilities and the nature of support will stimulate questioning as to how best the children are most likely to be motivated.

What Model of Support?

Traditionally, individual children's needs have been taken as the starting point. In any school, the support teacher is asked to work with individual children who are causing teachers to experience anxiety. Teachers may feel that the children need some form of special teaching, additional materials and teacher time. They may also wish to use the support teacher as a sounding board and as they seek confirmation that their practice is appropriate. Typical comments and requests made by teachers include:

'I worry so dreadfully about Ben. I want to find a way of boosting him before he gets entrenched in the feeling that he can't read.'

'Alex's mum feels like I do, that he's guessing and not really interested in his reading book.'

The support teacher needs to remain available, accessible and ready to work with individual children, as it is through mutual understanding and reciprocity that partnership can develop.

Tony Dessent (1987) suggests that the emphasis in working with individual children needs to shift from crisis intervention to carefully-planned patterns of support, reliable and rooted in availability. Class teachers require 'immediate access to advice, resources and materials at an early stage in the recognition of the problem, from a colleague who is close to hand'. However, support teachers need to be aware of the paradox of reinforcing isolationist tendencies by 'adapting' the curriculum through the use of individualized work programmes, simplified work sheets and so on; these may be seen as evidence of a child being 'slow' or 'behind'. Such children do not need a different diet to others. They need skilled teaching that takes into account their individual needs.

Much has been made of the geographical location of support – from corridor, cupboard, sick-room, to within the classroom. But the key issue is the underlying attitude, which should be positive, warm and inclusive. More often, working with an individual within the classroom can be a starting-point for including other children in a diverse range of activities. The hidden curriculum can be as powerful a determinant in acceptance as any overt behaviour on the part of the adults.

Evaluation and Observation

Arguably, the conventional emphasis on assessment and diagnosis tends to confirm what the class teacher *already* knows about the referred child. It may be a more positive and profitable use of the support teacher's time to carefully observe the child in various settings, in an attempt to identify how that child is understanding the range of experiences offered, their appropriateness, and their motivational content. In this way, subsequent support can be made available to the child through discussion, explanation and demonstration.

Evaluation based on *observation* and *interaction* with children engaged in tasks and *analysis* of their response, attitudes, motivation and confidence (whilst encouraging each piece of emergent behaviour) can form the basis of a child's profile. The question that must remain uppermost in the mind of the support teacher is 'How will the information gained be of practical use to the teacher and how will this help the child?' Sharing observations with the class teacher, non-teaching assistant and parent, followed by planning and agreeing responsibilities, lays the foundation on which a creative and positive framework of support can be built.

Many class teachers and support teachers jointly explore innovative ways of assessing and recording pupils' development and response, to enable and elicit further progress. Profiles, diaries and tape-recordings are increasingly used by all those responsible for the pupils' learning. Profiles include selected, dated examples of the childs work, for example:

- drawings;
- examples of unaided writing and subsequent drafts;
- writing for different purposes;
- 'books' made by the child;
- tape of the child telling a story;
- tape of the child sharing a story;
- tape of the child reading;
- tape of the child discussing a class or group project.

Some teachers encourage their pupils to become part of this selection process; in discussing and assembling a folder or profile, the teacher can feed back on and affirm progress. Such profiles can be used to discuss with parents stages that the child is moving through and form the basis for reviewing and planning further intervention.

Many class teachers use a diary format to record and relay information to parents (or any other supporting adults), particularly regarding reading behaviour. Home/school diaries can become valuable documents; not only do they provide a log of books shared by children/parents/siblings/grandparents or by adults/peers in school, but they may also serve as vehicles for exchanging queries about story interest, levels of competence, enjoyment and so on. Each adult working with an individual child can write down his or her observations and review the child's response. Class diaries can also become useful working documents in which planned support is clearly noted. They can be shared with professionals who may see the child less frequently (for example, educational psychologists or speech therapists) and will help to structure discussion on future support.

Developing Trust and Partnership

There are no magic answers, but a commitment to shared and equal responsibility is vital. Once relationships begin to develop, a tentative exploration of ownership of knowledge emerges. Trust can only be based on an awareness that class teachers may be apprehensive, and may well harbour deeply-hidden reservations about an 'expert', or 'specialist' working within their classroom. This insecurity may arise from past feelings of vulnerability at having to explain to parents why their child has not reached his or her expected potential. Many class teachers may have been working quietly, but determinedly, to support groups of children with a complex range of learning and/or emotional and behavioural difficulties but have become tired and demoralized by such efforts without adequate additional resourcing. A feeling of exploitation and resentment, fuelled by a continuous struggle for acknowledgement (or even mere survival) saps vital energy and goodwill.

Historically, teachers have worked in isolation and so they may feel exposed when another colleague is working in their domain. A readiness to verbalize differing perceptions and perspectives as to the right of the support person to 'intrude' in the complex organization of a school is fundamental to the development of a working partnership. This is especially important in curriculum development work, organization, emotional and behavioural development and working with parents and classroom assistants.

A continuous process of defining, negotiating and agreeing objectives and a willingness to share teaching tasks helps to create an affirmative climate. If the support teacher can respond to requests to work with a child, a group, or take the class group (thus enabling the class teacher to work with an individual or small group) then any trappings of mystique are soon discarded.

Ripple Effects

Creating opportunities for the *joint* exploration of reasons for a child's difficulty in learning helps alleviate anxieties of being professionally assessed and evaluated. Through such discussions, either party may be reminded of, or introduced to, alternative approaches which can be relevant to other children. An understanding of how children learn in ordinary classrooms involves careful analysis of practice. Headteachers, as well as support teachers, need to establish a climate which allows staff the opportunity to articulate the principles on which their practice is based. Those headteachers who genuinely aim for ongoing debate will build in time for class teachers to be freed for planning goals, reviewing resources and evaluating intervention. This continuous reassessment of perceived need and appropriate response also occurs in the classroom whilst working informally with groups of children or parents as well as on a more formal basis in staff meetings or case conferences.

Time is an important factor – for dialogue, for questions to emerge, for reflection, for practical support to develop. If priorities and goals are agreed and responsibilities allocated, awareness is sharpened and commitment heightened. There is a need to move away from the seductive simplicity of allocating blame for failure – 'within child', 'within group', 'within teacher', and begin to look at the interwoven strands that strengthen resolve and professional partnership.

Bettelheim suggests that 'most advice... is sought in the hope that it will confirm our prior convictions... We ask advice, but we mean approbation.' And: 'We cannot help mulling over the advice, being bothered by some of its aspects and intrigued by others.'

It is by developing shared responsibility that professionals can be stimulated to think out alternatives and options and to broaden choices in handling difficult challenges. Respect and recognition of adults' as well as of childrens' strengths is a very powerful force. Collaboration can engender tremendous energy and enthusiasm as the focus of support becomes clear and specific responsibilities are agreed. This is further enhanced when the individuals can focus on selected issues and set aside minor irritations resulting from differing perspectives.

Additional Attributes in Interprofessional Partnership

A support teacher needs to be able to make numerous and successive complex decisions in response to queries from a wide range of professionals as well as from children and parents. There are frequent changes in role and the support teacher needs to be able to make quick and accurate assessments of changing situations with full attention switched on to the impact on the recipient. If the support person is to be an effective communicator, he or she will need to assess the context, decide on the most appropriate ways of communicating and moniter what transpires. In order to maximize this communication with persons from different disciplines and power bases, the support teacher needs a working knowledge of the broader issues pertinent to his or her own field, as well as those with whom he or she is collaborating.

Such a role demands that the support teacher be open-minded, receptive, continuously seeking new approaches and reviewing lack of success as motivation to seek alternative methods. If the support proves unsuccessful on either side it should not be seen as evidence of a personal or professional failure, but as an indication of the need for a joint review to plan an alternative approach in the light of this experience.

In summary, support teachers must consider ways of:

- initiating and articulating policies;
- practical implementation;
- reviewing successes and difficulties;
- maintaining impetus;
- continuing a systematic and consistent approach.

Agreeing a Framework for Support

Interpersonal and interprofessional skills are vital attributes if support is going to be seen to be relevant to schools. A problem that continuously confronts support teachers however, is how to distribute effective support to all individuals, to all age-groups and to each curricular area. Tony Dessent (1987) argues that ordinary schools do not require an army of educational psychologists or advisory/peripatetic teachers to deliver their special expertise to individual children, for whom the schools are inadequately resourced and/or organized. A rationale for the work of external support staff can only develop within a context of resourcing and management which enables the headteacher and staff of the ordinary school to make appropriate responses to children with special needs. It is only within this framework that the support teacher can work in cooperation with ordinary teachers to develop skills and increase teacher sensitivity in order to respond to a wide range of individual differences amongst pupils.

Can the Supply Meet the Demand?

In a recent survey (Young, 1987) 92 per cent of the head teachers in East Oxfordshire primary schools stated that Special Needs Advisory and Support Teachers gave effective support to class teachers in their schools. A third of these, however, indicated that the support was *not* adequate to meet the needs of their school as a whole – if all teachers' concerns about children's learning or behaviour were to be addressed and if the support role was to be broadened. Eight per cent of head teachers said that a recurring problem was that of providing for children who were slow to develop in all areas of the curriculum. Seventy-eight per cent of class teachers who responded stated that Special Needs Advisory and Support Teachers (SNASTS) were not able to spend adequate time in each school to meet the needs of *all* children and that in many schools some groups of children were not being supported. This was regarded as unacceptable:

> With primary school class sizes at their present level, children with special needs will continue to struggle through an education system which is not designed for them. Special Needs Advisory and Support Teachers, with their present allocation of time, can be no more than a token gesture – the metaphorical finger in the dam.

A major issue confronting head teachers and support staff alike is that of finding ways to weave through the tangled web of conflicting attitudes, expectations, assumptions and values held by the different groups and individuals concerned in supporting a child with learning difficulties. This is made even more difficult by the diverse needs of the small group of special children in any school at a given time, who may have complex and continuing needs on the one hand and the majority of slower-learning children who may also present motivational or behavioural difficulties on the other. At present the support offered tends to lie in the hands of the generalist support teacher who may have limited expertise of children with specific and profound difficulties, such as visual, hearing, or serious physical difficulties. Tony Dessent (op.cit.) poses questions that haunt both support and mainstream school staff. These questions refuse to go away – for example, 'How do we make provision for exceptional needs at the end of the continuum?'; 'Why do we perpetuate the assumption that special needs are not self-evident – that they occur almost at random and need to be discovered and identified by teachers, educational psychologists and others?' 'Yet the majority group who are slow to learn and who pose a range of social/behavioural difficulties are relatively permanent and predictable products of our educational system.'

Effective Support

In the absence of a clear conceptual framework, support work runs the danger of drifting or lurching according to the educational and philosophical ideals of the individual. Those local education authorities who encourage support teams to use initiative and creativity in response to local need may be denying and evading their responsibility for devising a genuine support policy which takes into account the special needs of all children. Effective support requires local education authorities to make evident and explicit their policies and procedures. In addition, however, a structure which is able to offer clarity and direction for both support services *and* the recipients of that support is a factor that seems to be essential in the process of providing a more effective model of delivery.

'The learning opportunities open to the advisory and support teacher are manifold, both from partaking in a wealth of good practice and from experiencing the enthusiasm and commitment of head and class-teachers. However, it is necessary for support teachers to be given support' (Davies and Davies, 1988) to promote self-confidence, without which credibility with other professionals is unlikely to develop.

Chapter 4
Developing Support Systems for Young People with Special Needs in Secondary Schools

Hazel Bines

Approaches to special needs provision in the secondary school have changed considerably over the last ten years. The traditional focus on assessment and remedial tuition, which was particularly characteristic of the main form of special needs provision (that is, remedial education), has been extended to include a new cross-curricular and collaborative role for special needs teachers. Within this role, they may provide advice to subject teachers on learning materials and programmes and give support to pupils and teachers in mainstream teaching groups (Bines, 1986; Daniel, 1984; GB.DES, 1984; Hargreaves, 1984; Fish, 1985; Lavers, Pickup and Thomson, 1986; Lewis, 1984; Luton, 1986; Thomas and Jackson, 1986; Widlake, 1983). Encouraged by changes in secondary education, such as the growth of mixed ability teaching, moves to a common curriculum and a concern for equal opportunities and by the recognition that traditional approaches have often been too narrow and somewhat ineffective, a more egalitarian and integrative approach to special needs provision has been mooted. It is now accepted that all teachers should take some responsibility for special needs within the context of a 'whole school approach' and there is a new focus not just on individual pupil difficulties but also on the curricular and organizational changes which may be needed for more effective teaching and learning. Drawing on the useful analogy put forward by Golby and Gulliver there has been a shift from the provision of an 'ambulance service' for casualties of our current education system towards a new emphasis on the importance of 'road safety'.

Views on how this new approach should be developed and implemented have been somewhat varied, given the range of individual schools, pupil needs and extant practices which it encompasses. Nevertheless, certain common and salient features can be discerned. Of particular importance is the extended role of the special needs teacher, which has been usefully summarized by the National Association for Remedial Education as comprising assessment, prescription, teaching, advice and support to subject and class teachers, liaison, coordination and the development and management of a whole school policy towards special educational needs and provision (NARE, 1985). This implies changes in the clientele, context, content and expertise associated with remedial and other special educational provision (Bines, (op.cit). Special needs teachers may well be concerned with a far broader spectrum of pupil needs as the context of special needs work moves from traditional withdrawal or special classes focusing on basic skills towards the whole curriculum and mainstream teaching groups. Content may frequently include subject as well as basic skills and knowledge as pupils are given help across the curriculum and special needs teachers apply their diagnostic and teaching knowledge to mainstream curricula and teaching methods. This in turn will need new expertise, for example on the learning difficulties which may be experienced by pupils in different subjects and the ways in which they can be successfully taught in large, mainstream (and frequently mixed ability) teaching groups. Special needs teachers will also need new interpersonal skills to foster the collaborative 'partnership' between special needs and subject or class teacher and will also need new management skills to develop whole-school provision and policies.

Such changes are also beginning to mould the work not only of special needs teachers within individual secondary schools but also the work of former peripatetic remedial and other services. Such remedial services in particular are being encouraged to move *from* a model of individual teaching and support, *towards* one including advisory help for teachers and involvement in mainstream classes, both in the primary and the secondary sector. In some cases, their work is being complemented or extended by support teacher services for emotional and behavioural difficulties and for sensory impairment (Barnsley Special Education Team, 1981; Gipps, Gross and Goldstein, 1987; Goodwin, 1983; Fish (1985a); Laskier, 1985;

Moses, Hegarty and Jowett, 1987). In addition, special schools are changing their role, fostering links and integration programmes with mainstream schools and acting as advisory and resource centres (Dessent, 1984; Hallmark, 1983; Fish 1985a; Moses *et al.* 1987, op.cit.). Within secondary schools a range of special provision is beginning to be provided, including special classes and units and also 'resource rooms' and other more integrated approaches (Jones and Berrick, 1985). There has thus been a distinct shift in the conception of special needs provision and of service delivery, which moreover has been given considerable encouragement and policy support at both local and national level. Following the Warnock Report (Warnock, 1978) (which crystallized and developed changes in thinking about special needs provision, arguing for a wider concept of special educational needs and for more flexible approaches to provision) and the 1981 Education Act (which recognized that all teachers should take some reponsibility for special needs), there has since been further endorsement of the cross-curricular advisory and support approach by HMI (GB.DES, 1984b). LEAs have also begun to encourage such developments (for example; Hargreaves, 1984; Fish, 1985).

The advantages of this new model appear to be considerable. Pupils who may formerly have been withdrawn for special needs help or have been placed in a special class (or, indeed, a special school) should be able to enjoy the academic and social benefits of greater integration enhanced by the support and by greater expertise and commitment from subject teachers. Subject teachers should be able to gain from the sharing of ideas and methods and from having help and advice, whilst special needs teachers should have a more stimulating and challenging role and be less isolated from their mainstream colleagues. Schools will have a clearly thought-out 'whole school policy' with agreed principles and properly planned assessment, monitoring, liaison and resources. Both experience and research would suggest that such benefits may well be forthcoming. It has been suggested, for example, that pupils' learning experiences will be broadened and self-esteem increased whilst teachers can become more sensitive to pupils' special needs and develop confidence in their teaching expertise (Lavers *et al.*, op.cit.). Help may also be provided for such teaching problems as not having enough time for individuals in large teaching groups and benefiting pupil and teacher; special needs teachers in turn can find their new role both more stimulating and more effective (Bines, op.cit.).

Although much attention has been given to these advantages of the new approach and to the organizational and role aspects of a cross-curricular support and advisory approach, there has been less consideration of policy aims, of processes and outcomes, of difficulties of implementation and of future directions. There are a number of issues and problems involved. These are now being increasingly recognized as the practicalities of change, which are experienced as the support model becomes more refined. The degree to which this new model has been implemented is debatable. Two fairly recent surveys, for example, found that although special needs teachers were involved with assessment, special group teaching and liaison with parents and extra-school agencies, there were few instances of such teachers working alongside their subject colleagues (Clunies-Ross and Wimhurst, 1983; GB.DES, 1984b). Similarly, the role of extra-school support services had not always moved to a supportive and advisory model (Gipps *et al.*, op.cit.). It would also seem that integration from special schools has not been as substantial as might have been expected and in some instances specialized provision has increased – notably, the provision of offsite units for 'disruptive' pupils (Booth, 1981; Swann, 1987). It would thus seem that much needs to be done to successfully develop the new model. In particular, it could be argued, three major areas require considerable debate and analysis. The first involves *'support'*, including what it should comprise and how it can be successfully developed; the second, *policy*, particularly 'whole school' and LEA policies; and the third, the *momentum and context* of change – that is, how support services can continue to respond to pupil, teacher and school needs and to current and future developments in the curricula, teaching methods and organization of secondary education. These three areas will now each be briefly considered.

Developing support

Although support is central to this new model it is only now being recognized that it may be a problematic concept. As Visser (1986) has argued that if support is not to depreciate (as past terminology has done) then there must be a clearer view of what is entailed. Currently, support would appear to take a number of forms, including supporting individual *pupils* (both in small groups and in mainstream classes) and supporting *teachers* (with advice and help on materials and methods and through assistance in the classroom). Each of these aspects of support would seem to be an important part of a special needs teacher's role. However, as Hart (1986) has pointed out in a very useful analysis, support work may actually be based on some very different conceptions of pupil needs, curriculum, provision and change. Some support teachers will tend to emphasize what Hart calls the 'individual approach', focusing on individual pupil difficulties and ensuring that the curriculum provided is adapted and matched accordingly. Support work will thus largely comprise identifying and helping individuals, providing them with additional materials and equipment and evaluating individual progress. The 'whole curriculum approach', in contrast, is based on the assumption that schools can do much to prevent special needs and that what is primarily needed is change in the curriculum for *all* children to make learning more appropriate and effective including for those with special needs. Work will thus focus on planning for, and teaching, the whole class and adapting classroom practice in general (ibid., pp. 26–28).

Of course it could be agreed that ideally neither of these models are incompatible, in that the process of helping individuals should also generate ways of extending the expertise of class teachers and making curricula and pedagogy more appropriate and effective for all pupils. However such an assumption ignores the many constraints on the development of support work. In particular, most support teams, whether based in special needs departments or in extra-school services, are likely to have only limited staffing and resources at their disposal, making it almost impossible to provide a level of individual support which will 'saturate' schools and classrooms to the degree required to develop subject and class teachers' expertise through work on materials and teaching methods, through teaching example, team teaching and evaluation and through departmental and whole school in-service and discussion sessions. This in turn may impinge on the amount of attention which can be given to the needs of specific individuals, both in a particular class when working with the class teacher and when considering how staffing is to be deployed in general throughout the school (for example, whether it is to be used for *small group* tuition of very poor readers or be given instead to developing better teaching materials with a particular *department*). Choices will have to be made about what is the most effective way to work. It would seem that the 'whole curriculum approach' is likely to be most productive in terms of long-term change (Hart, ibid.; Hockley, 1985; Visser, op.cit.), but nevertheless far more consideration needs to be given to the aims and assumptions of different models of support, the resources available to implement them and the consequences of adopting particular emphases and orientations.

This would seem to be more important when other constraints on support work are also considered: namely, teacher expectations and expertise. In particular, it has often been too blandly assumed that with the right approach from special needs teachers, subject and class teachers will accept the new cross-curricular support and advisory model and see its benefits to both pupils and themselves. Lewis, for example, (amongst others) has suggested that if what is offered is relevant and practical, the confidence of colleagues will be won and attitudes will be changed (Lewis, 1984, p.11). Whilst this may be the case in many instances, other experiences would suggest that the outcome of support and collaboration may be less positive. Ferguson and Adams (1982), for example, found that remedial support teachers were often relegated to being teacher's aides with no real role to play. My own research (Bines, op. cit.) also highlighted such problems, with remedial teachers feeling they sometimes had little power to change curricula and teaching methods and subject teachers considering that special needs support should be limited to helping those with learning difficulties and not extended to the rest of the class and the whole curriculum. As Hart (op.cit.) and Vissar (op.cit.) have also noted, it is only too easy for support to become limited and static. Given past models of special needs provision, it is going to take time to change views and expectations. It also needs to be recognized that not all subject teachers will necessarily welcome collaboration, perhaps feeling their competence or their 'territory' is threatened. In addition, particularly if special needs teachers do attempt wider curriculum change, there may be conflict about teaching content and methods (Bines, op.cit.). It is also important to acknowledge that if such problems can be experienced by school-based staff, and in relation to pupils whose difficulties are relatively mild, then there is every possibility that collaboration may be even more difficult for extra-school services and special school staff and where pupils' handicaps may require considerably more change and adjustment. It may also be questionable whether special needs staff have appropriate experience for cross-curricular work and collaboration. There is some doubt as to required experience and whether special needs teachers have it (see Visser, 1986; Widlake, 1983; Bines, 1986).

'Support' thus raises a number of problems as well as advantages. Nevertheless, analysis and experience suggest there are a number of strategies and approaches which can be adopted. Above all it would seem that much care and time needs to be devoted to change, recognizing the importance of modifying attitudes and overcoming anxieties, particularly through good communications and an atmosphere of trust. There also needs to be careful planning, both of individual support sessions (so that each teacher knows his or her responsibilities) and of overall resources and provision. A systematic programme of advisory and support work should be established, working with certain years and/or departments in turn to ensure effectiveness, with link teachers being established in each department or faculty to continue work on curricula and contribute to the overall coordination of cross-curricular development. Timetabling also needs to be considered, particularly the advantages of 'blocking' so that support can be systematic and more economic, and it is also important to develop parental involvement. Careful use of ancillary helpers as well as support teachers would also seem to be an essential part of such planning, with due regard for ways in which several adults can work together in the classroom (Edwards, op.cit.; Lavers *et al.*, op.cit.; Luton, op.cit.; Smith, 1982; Thomas, 1986). My own research (Bines, op.cit.) would also suggest that it is important to consider not only what special needs teachers may wish to achieve but also the perceptions and concerns of subject teachers, in particular their views on the content and teaching of subjects and the problems of managing large teaching groups, including pupils with special needs. In addition, assessments used should reflect skills and knowledge required across the curriculum and there should be an inbuilt programme of evaluation, both of individual and group pupil progress and of the value and effectiveness of support and advisory work (Bines, ibid.). This approach thus requires very careful planning, allied to a 'whole school policy', which will now be discussed.

Developing policy

Like 'support', the concept of a 'whole school policy' or 'whole school approach' has been given wide credence as a means of change but little detailed consideration as to what it entails and how it should be developed and implemented. It is now, however, being given some attention. Butt, for example, has suggested that the whole school approach means that every effort is made to 'normalize' and integrate those with special needs, with all staff taking responsibility and special needs provision being directed towards a curriculum support role rather than an exclusively child-centred one (Butt, 1986, pp.10-11). Roaf (1986), taking a slightly wider view, has suggested that whole school policies particularly associated with equal opportunities and human rights (including special needs) are the means of establishing a particular ethos or goal: that is, principles about education. A 'whole school policy' on special needs would thus seem to be concerned both with the aims and ethos of provision and with means of realization, through stressing the responsibility of all staff and the need for cooperation and curriculum change.

Such a policy could also be seen as offering guidelines for curriculum, teaching methods and organization and/or as a codification of established practice. It could comprise a set of unwritten assumptions, but may equally take some documentary form. However there seem to be few, if any, examples of written policies, or accounts of how they were developed. Rather, a whole school policy seems largely to have been regarded as the implementation of the cross-curricular advisory and support approach, a policy demonstrated via practice and discussion rather than through written aims and guidelines. Nor is it entirely clear how all staff should be involved in the making of such a policy or how prescriptive it should be.

It could be argued, however, that a more explicit and documented approach to policy development has a number of advantages. It could, for example, help to clarify the aims and goals of support across the curriculum in a particular school. It could also help to delineate priorities, for instance the areas of the curriculum most in need of change, or what teaching approaches and organization should be encouraged. It could also be used to suggest how special needs and other staff might work together and the lines of responsibility and management which should be established and developed in relation to such issues as assessment, liaison with extra-school agencies and parental involvement. Outlining a policy could be a particularly useful preliminary exercise for special needs teachers themselves; it could then be used as a mechanism of change, through staff working parties and departmental and whole staff discussion to develop the policy. Different views on approaches and priorities might then be identified (and possibly resolved) before they impinged on practice. At least all staff would then be aware of the issues and problems involved in providing for special needs. Strategies and planning, such as discussed in the last section, could then be related to each aspect of the policy, so that general aims, principles and ways of working could be translated into daily practice. It could also be used for deciding and planning resource allocation, including staffing. Finally it could also be a useful tool for evaluating curricula and teaching methods and the effectiveness of support and other aspects of change which have been implemented, thus acting as a continuously dynamic reflection of the growth and development of a school's provision and response.

Such a model policy development would seem to reflect the cooperative approach to change in attitudes and practice which is presumed in the support and advisory approach to special needs provision. It might also facilitate the greater involvement of extra-school services. Members of such services could well contribute to aspects of such a policy by participating in discussion, by offering particular specialist expertise (for example of sensory impairments and their implications for provision) and, perhaps above all, by bringing their knowledge of practice in other schools to bear on particular issues or problems. It has already been suggested that one problem for such services concerns the legitimacy of their involvement focused on support: participation in policy processes, once established, with some concomitant responsibility for implementation and outcomes, might begin to break down barriers between 'school' and 'extra school' staff. A similar point could be made about the staff of special schools working in increasing collaboration with mainstream schools, particularly if this collaboration is enhanced by and grounded in individual and collective integration programmes concerning pupils in both schools.

Such whole school policies would then need to be linked to LEA and national policy-making. Understandably perhaps, much recent LEA policy-making in the area of special educational needs has focused on the implementation of the 1981 Education Act and its many procedures. However if the support and advisory model is to be successfully developed in an LEA's schools, far more attention will have to be given to policy process than has been the case to date, in particular to policy congruence, to resources and to LEA-wide initiatives and support for schools. In respect to policy congruence it would seem to be essential that both schools and their LEAs are committed to a similar policy direction and that it is not just assumed that an authority's policies will be reflected in schools, particularly since research in other policy fields such as multicultural education would suggest that an authority's policies may be misunderstood, only partially implemented or even ignored and this is a field which has often had a considerably higher policy profile that special needs. The development of policy at individual school level could mutually facilitate both school and LEA policy congruence and implementation. It could help to identify what is considered to be 'good practice' by the authority's schools for consideration by the LEA. It could in turn be used to elevate the degree to which a particular school has responded to LEA policy initiatives and requirements. Equally, it would seem that more attention should be given to developing an understanding of resource implications – because of the range of special needs which may be presented by pupils and which may require specialist expertise which it is not always appropriate nor possible for staff or individual schools to have, and because of the heavy demands on staffing which support can make. In addition, change of the type now being mooted, with its immense ramifications for the whole curriculum, pedagogy and organization of a school, often needs support which can only be provided by the broader and greater resources available to LEAs as opposed to individual schools. The momentum and debate which has been generated by the Fish Report (Fish, 1985) is one example of how LEAs could help to generate change: Butt's account of an in-service initiative, albeit on a smaller scale, provides a further instance of how the sharing of ideas and practice on an authority-wide basis can be similarly effective (Butt, 1986).

Such regular policy review between an LEA and its schools and LEA support and involvement could be further strengthened by area support services disseminating practice and giving appropriate help, resources and support. To be effective, however, they will have to become more unified, particularly for secondary schools where lines of responsibility and management are necessarily complex, given the numbers of pupils and staff involved and the many and varied demands on the secondary curriculum and organization. However, despite the recommendations of the Warnock Report it would seem that progress towards a generic, unified service has been slow (Moses *et al.*, 1987) even without the wider problem of incorporating health authority-based services such as speech therapy and physiotherapy. Perhaps now that the full implications of developing a cross-curricular, advisory and support model are beginning to be recognized, more attention will be paid to such issues.

However, even with such improvements, a number of problems will still need to be resolved. For example it may not be easy to establish a consensus of views and practice, either in individual schools or between schools and LEA. There is also the issue of the degree to which any policy, at school or LEA level, should be prescriptive as well as enabling, and how both schools and LEAs should respond to national policy initiatives and developments. However with greater attention to policy process as an aspect of change, such issues could at least be debated. Moreover there would then be greater opportunities to evaluate future developments, some of which will now be briefly considered in conclusion.

Future Trends and Developments

It has been argued that although the support and advisory model could now be considered to be the model of 'good practice' for special needs provision, further analysis and planning are still required, particularly in relation to developing and managing collaboration and change. Nor can it be assumed that because the new approach apparently has many advantages that it will necessarily be accepted in practice, or successfully implemented. The wide remit involved, from the initiation of a cooperative relationship between subject and special needs teacher in an individual classroom through to the establishment of a unified support service at authority level, will necessarily make great demands on an overstretched service which is also having to cope with readjustments to its own practices and assumptions.

Nevertheless the secondary sector does offer a number of opportunities for change and development. Unlike most of their colleagues in the primary sector, special needs teachers in secondary schools are likely to have the flexibility of teaching role which enables them to work alongside colleagues in classrooms and departments. In addition, mainstream secondary staff face many demands, such as realizing curricular expectations in large classes with a range of pupil attainments and dispositions, which may make them receptive to the benefits of support and advice. Moreover, although curriculum and pastoral structures may sometimes be complex, they do provide established lines of communication and responsibilities to facilitate working with support services and the development of policy at various management levels within the school. Secondary schools have also been an arena for change in recent years, and should be open to new ideas and practices.

The effective use of such a potentially fertile context of change will, however, require a greater awareness and responsiveness from support teachers than has been the case with the new model of special provision discussed here, which has taken over ten years to be developed, implemented and evaluated (and implementation and evaluation is far from complete). The place of the secondary sector at the problematic interface of school, work (or unemployment) and society is likely to continue to result in a continuing pattern of new initiatives, each with their particular implications for special provision. It also needs to be recognized that this new model of practice concerns and requires the maintenance and development of egalitarian and comprehensive principles for secondary schooling, which may not be easy to sustain given the continuing pressures on secondary education (Bines, 1986) and the future life chances likely to be accorded to those seen to have special needs in an increasingly complex and technological society also faced with structural youth unemployment (Tomlinson, 1985). Past changes in secondary education encouraged a new and enhanced role for special provision. It cannot be assumed, however, that future curricular and policy changes will be so facilitative. Special needs support teachers will have to continue to ensure that policy attention and resources are given to special needs provision, that their role remains both central and innovative and that future initiatives enhance rather than constrain the gains which have been made for young people with special needs. Currently, for example, the development of GCSE is posing a number of problems for the successful integration of those with special needs in the examination years of schooling, yet insufficient debate has taken place on this issue. TVEI is another development within which the role of special educators, if any, has hardly been considered and (somewhat paradoxically perhaps) a similar comment could be made about the Lower Attaining Pupils Project (LAPP) (GB.DES, 1986b). The HMI report (GB.DES, 1986) makes no real mention of special needs teachers' involvement in the LAPP projects.

Much more thought must thus be given to developments in examinations and training, to other changes such as a national curriculum, to the role of special education within equal opportunities policies (Bines, op.cit.) and to social and economic changes which are having (or may yet have) their effects on education (cf. Widlake, 1983). Special education services in the secondary sector have at last, perhaps, largely moved from their former neglected isolation towards a potentially effective and professional model. Future development now requires the extension of professional, educational and political awareness and expertise to ensure that this model does indeed become and continue to be an important and innovative aspect of secondary education.

Chapter 5
Local and Regional Variations in Support

Jim Conway

The idea of having unattached teachers to support children with special educational needs (SEN) is not new: in 1889 the Royal Commission on the Blind and Deaf envisaged that children who were blind would be taught 'in ordinary classes by ordinary teachers' and 'in town schools special instruction in reading might be given by visiting teachers' (quoted in Warnock, 1978). By this time a specialist teacher was already visiting ordinary schools in Cardiff and the London Home Teaching Society had since 1873 been sending teachers to visit London's National Schools to teach children who were blind (Pritchard, 1963).

After a consideration of the range of support services now to be found in most Local Education Authorities (LEAs) I will delineate some changes which are currently taking place. Following this I will describe the development of support teacher services in my own Authority. Finally I will address some of the issues which I consider to be central to any debate on the future development of support services. These issues have emerged during discussions with children, parents, class teachers, head teachers, support teachers and other colleagues and following reflection on my experience of helping to establish and reorganize support services in two LEAs.

Support Services

Most support teacher services are still identified by disability type, such as hearing impairment or visual impairment. Gipps, Gross and

Goldstein (1987) found that 97 per cent of LEAs have a service for the (rather difficult to define) group of pupils who are said to have learning difficulties. One third of the LEAs which completed their questionnaire still call their service the 'Remedial Service' although many services have been renamed (probably because of the changing terminology in use in special needs since the Warnock Report and the implementation of the 1981 Education Act). Gipps, Gross and Goldstein discovered that new names for this service produced a list of 35 alternative titles, most including the words 'support' or 'advisory'.

Traditionally, remedial services identified children (often only in primary schools) who had learning difficulties in reading, writing and spelling and then visited the schools on a regular basis to teach those children in groups withdrawn from their regular classes. Moses *et al.* (1987) found that two-thirds of the 77 authorities they surveyed reported major innovations in their support services. They identified four characteristics common to these new services: concern with a *wider range* of learning difficulties; an extension of responsibility to *all age groups*; working with *teachers as well as pupils* and working with pupils *in the classroom* more often than in a withdrawal situation.

Gipps, Gross and Goldstein (op.cit.) found a wide variation in the number of staff employed in support services for children with reading and other learning difficulties; 18 per cent of LEAs had five or less while another 18 per cent of LEAs had over 40. Although there was a tendency for the largest LEAs to have the biggest services there were exceptions: four of the smallest authorities had 21 or more support staff and two of the largest had ten or fewer.

Although support services for children who have impaired hearing appear to exist in every LEA, there are still a number of authorities which do not have a service to support children who have a visual impairment. Advisory and support staff for the hearing impaired offer teachers technical advice on the use of special aids such as the radio microphone (phonic ear) and provide advice on teaching methods and classroom organization to teachers who have within their classes children with impaired hearing. Similarly, teachers of the visually impaired offer technical advice on low vision aids, which may include closed circuit television systems, and guidance on classroom organization and teaching methods. Both of these services usually support pupils in special schools as well as in primary and secondary schools, pre-school children and students in further education.

Few LEA's have a support service for children who have physical disabilities. Support for these children should ideally come from a team of staff, possibly including the school doctor, occupational therapist, a specialist teacher and perhaps a physiotherapist. As with children who have a hearing impairment, schools may require the services of a speech therapist. Schools are likely to need information and advice on the educational and social implications of specific disabilities, advice on furniture and equipment, support and advice for specific learning difficulties and perhaps help with programmes of physical exercises and speech and language development.

A more recent type of support service provides help with emotional and behaviour difficulties. The objectives and organization of one service has been described as an attempt to counter the trend towards segregated provision in the form of disruptive units (Coulby, 1986). It has been suggested that this is perhaps one of the most difficult areas of advisory and support teaching because the causes of these difficulties may include poor class management and the children involved may challenge the authority of teachers (Fish, 1985). This challenge might disrupt lessons, provoking feelings of both guilt and anger in the teacher and interfering with the learning of other pupils.

A service which often plays a major role in the assessment and support of pupils with emotional and behaviour problems is the psychological service. Although having a major role in the assessment of special educational needs, educational psychologists also have important responsibilities in offering support for some pupils, in the support of individual teachers and in in-service education generally. Like the service for children with impaired hearing or impaired vision, educational psychologists regularly work with pre-school children and often with students beyond the age of 16.

Between January 1981 and October 1986, the number of educational psychologists employed by LEAs increased by 40 per cent. Although most of this increase can be attributed to the effects of the 1981 Act, other reasons include the increased training responsibilities of psychologists, increased involvement with Social Services and District Health Authorities and the development of Portage home teaching services (Association of Educational Psychologists, 1987). The 104 LEAs now employ over 1400 educational psychologists. As with other services, psychologists are not evenly distributed across the population. In my own region of Yorkshire and Humberside the ratio of psychologists to school population in 1985 varied from 1:9,600 to 1:5,000.

The educational welfare or educational social work service also provides a wide range of advice and practical support to children with special educational needs (SEN) and their parents. As well as intervening in cases of irregular school attendance and lateness, the educational social worker (ESW) has functional responsibilities in respect of the provision of free school meals and school uniform and in the preparation of reports for Juvenile Court. Educational social workers often act as the link between schools and social workers from an authority's social services department. They may also link with school doctors and health visitors employed by the District Health Authority (DHA), which also provides a range of paramedical services to support children in school, including speech therapy, physiotherapy and occupational therapy.

There is considerable variation between authorities in the organization and provision of support services for children with SEN. These differences can usually be attributed to a combination of historical, political and fiscal factors.

Recent changes in LEA support services

Following a nationwide survey, Goacher *et al.* (1987) reported that 52 per cent of LEAs recorded a substantial increase in the number of peripatetic advisory and support teachers employed for special educational needs between 1983 and 1986 while only two per cent recorded a substantial decrease. At the same time 23 per cent of LEAs recorded a substantial decrease in their numbers of special school teachers. This would appear to suggest that some authorities may be shifting the emphasis in their special educational provision from institutionally based services (in special schools) to advisory and support services. Gipps *et al.* op.cit.) suggest that advisory and support services were undergoing considerable change in the early 1980s. Hart (1986) maintains that one of the main developments in special educational provision in recent years has been the widespread introduction of in-class support teaching in secondary schools as an alternative to withdrawal groups and remedial classes.

My own experience in helping to re-model and develop support services in two LEAs, plus a limited knowledge of what is happening in a number of other authorities, suggests that the same change has been taking place in primary schools.

Support teachers intervene in classrooms to support children or teachers or both. Gipps and Goldstein (1984) identified a move towards supporting the class teacher rather than the child. More recently, Gipps *et al.* (op.cit.) confirmed that the main change in LEA models of support for special needs in the ordinary school was a move towards having the class teacher as the client of the support services rather than the child. By 1983 they identified fifteen LEAs where this change had taken place. In their survey of 77 LEA Support Services, Moses *et al.* (op.cit.) found that in two LEAs services were directed exclusively towards teachers; in another two their clients were exclusively pupils, while in the rest support teachers divided their time between teachers and pupils. In 63 per cent of the services, support teachers spent at least half their time teaching.

While many LEAs have developed most, if not all, of the support teacher services described earlier, until recently it was uncommon to find in an authority a single coherent management structure for all the services. The fragmentation of the teacher support services in many LEAs was criticized in the Warnock Report, which suggested that the provision of advice to schools on children with SEN should be coordinated. It recommended that every LEA should unify its support services.

An increasingly important feature of provision for children with SEN in primary and secondary schools is the classroom assistant. It is common practice in many LEAs to appoint non-teaching assistants (NTAs) to support individual pupils. Goacher *et al.* (op.cit.) found that 76 per cent of LEAs reported a substantial increase since 1983 in the number of classroom or welfare assistants they employed. In some authorities, these assistants are engaged on temporary contracts and are sometimes given little or no training. In my own LEA the great majority of assistants are qualified nursery nurses. NTAs are appointed where children have toiletting or mobility problems. They are all appointed centrally to a team of Curriculum Support Assistants (established in 1985 as part of the Curriculum Support Service) and are offered regular in-service training. They are deployed by the Assistant Education Officer (AEO) (SEN) and are responsible on a day-to-day basis to the head teacher of the school in which they work. To help schools make the most effective use of this new type of service, the authority has issued guidance to schools on the role of the Curriculum Support Assistant.

Teacher support services in one LEA

Like many LEAs, my own Authority developed a number of teacher support services during the 1970s in response to specific pressures and needs. Teachers were appointed with different conditions of service, salary structures and management systems. In 1974 the authority appointed its first peripatetic teacher of the hearing impaired. This service now includes a specialist pre-school teacher, a primary school teacher and a teacher who works in special schools, secondary schools, and colleges of further education. At different times the head of service has been responsible to the Principal Educational Psychologists, Senior Assistant Education Officer (Primary and Special Education), the Adviser and the Assistant Education Officer (Special Educational Needs).

Since 1974 the LEA has deployed three teachers as educational home visitors. They work in the homes of children prior to their admission to nursery class or school. This service is in the process of being remodelled and expanded to provide support for more children of pre-school age who have SEN. In 1979 the LEA appointed a specialist teacher to support children who were visually impaired. In the same year, in response to national and local concern about disruption in schools and as an alternative to the increasingly popular practice of opening 'disruptive units', the LEA established an education support team. Six teachers were appointed including a team leader who was responsible to the Senior Assistant Education Officer (Secondary). The team was given the task of helping secondary schools support children with emotional and behavioural problems.

In response to the 1981 Act and in support of schools which were maintaining in regular classes a wider range of children, including those said to have 'moderate learning difficulties', the LEA established in 1985 the Curriculum Support Service. Curriculum Support Teachers offer direct teaching to some children and advice and resources to teachers. The title was chosen to emphasize the importance of the curriculum in the creation of learning difficulties.

Since 1984, experienced and knowledgeable teachers and other staff from a special school have provided advice and support for children with physical disabilities in primary and secondary schools. In particular, a teacher of primary aged children devotes much of her week to offering advice and help on the learning difficulties of children with physical disabilities. A specialist PE teacher runs in-service courses and visits primary and secondary schools to offer advice on the integration of children with physical disabilities into regular PE classes. An occupational therapist and three physiotherapists based at the school are also part of this support team. However, Fish (op.cit.) suggests that support services such as this for children with physical disabilities are seldom available.

Given the range of support services within an education department in addition to medical and paramedical services, social services, probation service, etc., which may offer advice on the management and education of one child, it is not surprising that teachers are sometimes puzzled by inconsistencies in the advice from different support staff. Like a number of authorities in recent years, this LEA has drawn together the teacher support services under a common management structure and provided a single, central base to encourage coordination and cooperation. Moses *et al.* (op.cit.) report that one-fifth of LEAs claimed to have combined separate support services into a single service. However, I would suggest that the coordination of services in itself does not solve all of the social and professional problems associated with support work or answer the questions raised by the assumptions which underpin it. In the last part of this chapter I will identify and discuss some of the questions and issues highlighted by the nature of support work and the nature of the relationship between the supported and the supporter.

'Not with a class of 29': issues in support work

Although the issues I discuss in this section are to do with support teaching, I hope the discussion has a wider application and offers some insight into the relationships between many advice givers, particularly those from outside school such as psychologists, advisers or inspectors, medical and paramedical staff, and many advice receivers.

When Tony Dessent (1985) asked himself the question 'Do we know how to support children with special needs in ordinary schools?', his answer was that 'We do *not* know how'! Perhaps the situation is not quite as bleak as he indicates. I would suggest that what is needed is a response from authorities to demands for support for children with SEN, which in some cases is rather more studied than hitherto and which is grounded in the reality and experiences of practitioners and the social worlds of the classroom and staffroom. I will attempt to address some of the social and professional issues raised by the notion of support work.

Despite the rich variety in the nature, organization and size of support services, these issues are almost invariably raised during any discussion of support work and may be fundamental to any support situation. Some of them are to do with assumptions which underpin this type of work. For example, in many teacher support services there is a taken-for-granted assumption that another adult, often an outsider, can intervene effectively in the social world of the classroom to the benefit of a child. Is there always careful consideration of the effect of this action on the class teacher, other children and the child concerned? Who find outs what the class teacher really feels about being supported? Does anyone offer an adequate explanation to the target child, and other children, for this intrusion?

There is considerable debate about the value of working with the class teacher instead of, or as well as, with the child. Many support teachers argue that this is a more effective form of intervention. They may work with class teachers in planning, teaching and follow-up activities. What are the role and training implications of this change for the support teacher? The large number of teachers and schools with which many support teachers have to work makes this style of work difficult. Are there alternative patterns of work to the regular visit? Perhaps the support teacher can target attention on a limited number of teachers or schools for a specified period? I will concern myself with five major issues: the knowledge and skills required by support teachers; the relationship between support teacher and class teacher; the question of where support teachers should be based and accountability and evaluation.

The knowledge and skills required by support teachers
If support staff are to work increasingly with class teachers rather than children, which skills and what sort of knowledge do they need

to make those professional relationships productive? The skills required to intervene in *classrooms* – advising teachers on teaching method, classroom organization and resources – are not the skills needed by support teachers who teach children *individually* or in small groups. They need to be able to approach other teachers in a manner which quickly fosters warm and trusting relationships, to communicate clearly, negotiate effectively and resolve conflict sensitively. They need to be able to share their expertise. The difficulties faced by many remedial teachers who are expected to undergo a transformation and emerge as support teachers were demonstrated by Bailey (1981). Following a survey of 20 heads of remedial departments, he found they were either reluctant or considered they lacked the expertise to give advice or to work alongside colleagues in the classroom. The skills required by support teachers depend to some extent on personal qualities. In my experience, support teachers are selected because of their interpersonal skills as much as their knowledge of, and ability to provide for, special educational needs.

However, support teachers must have knowledge of classroom management, use of teaching resources, curriculum planning and meeting individual needs. In my view, this can only be acquired during experience of teaching in the phase of education in which they are asked to provide support, and perhaps as the result of extensive study undertaken informally on a personal basis or by following a substantial course of in-service training. However, I have worked with a number of teachers who are very knowledgeable yet have no formal additional qualifications. Their knowledge comes from informed and intelligent reflection on classroom practice and a lively interest in children and their learning.

The relationship between class teacher and support teacher
Appropriate experience and knowledge will help ensure the credibility of a support teacher. However, the perceived and actual status of the support teacher will do much to structure the role relationship between support teacher and *supported* teacher. There is a significant difference between being presented or presenting oneself as an 'expert' as opposed to a colleague who has chosen to specialize in supporting other teachers in meeting special educational needs by sharing their problems. As an expert one may be expected to be very knowledgeable and able to offer solutions to

problems others find intractable. Perhaps class teachers are too willing to believe in the 'myth of the expert', as their involvement may
transfer ownership of the problem and allow the class teacher to
concentrate efforts on the 'other twenty-nine'. The failure of an
'expert' to solve a problem can lead to feelings of hopelessness, dis-
illusionment and frustration for the class teacher. Dessent (op.cit.)
suggests experts have the following characteristics: they are highly
trained, few in number and gaining access to them is next to impossible! A head teacher from a nearby LEA complained to me that
the support service in his authority was a 'waste of money' because
it was 'all chiefs and no indians'. The service contained a larger-
than-usual proportion of teachers paid on Scale Four and above.
Perhaps this structure made the support teachers' relationships with
class teachers more difficult?

On the other hand being a fellow teacher of similar status and
having common professional and career interests, perhaps even
sharing a staffroom culture, provides a different framework for the
relationship. It is reasonable to assume that the salary scale and title
assigned to support teachers by an LEA would be significant factors in the definition of status. One would also assume that the
choice of allowance and title are reflections of the prevalent perception of the role of support teachers within an LEA. My own
research (Conway, 1987) indicates that two of the main functions
of special needs administrative and support services are to help
LEAs meet statutory obligations and to implement procedures by
which resources at the margin are allocated equitably. Are support
teachers employed primarily to limit the number of candidates put
forward for expensive special educational provision? If that is the
intention, it certainly didn't work out that way in one LEA (Goodwin, 1983). I would suggest that most support teachers feel they
are employed to help teachers help children. The case against the
support teacher being portrayed as an 'expert' would appear to have
been well made by Dessent and others. Nevertheless, the specialist
knowledge and skills of the support teacher should be recognized.
What evidence is there to support the view that the support teacher
who is perceived as a peer and who has *specialist* as opposed to
general classroom skills may be more successful than the support
teacher perceived as an 'expert'?

In a study of behaviour at work, Blau (1964) found that individuals
prefer to consult colleagues with whom they have friendly relations

than consult an 'expert'. Both Homans (1972) and Blau (op.cit.) recognize that the potential cost of seeking advice in the work situation is the acknowledgement of inferiority, unless the help and advice is reciprocated. To this end, Blau found that staff turned for help to colleagues nearly like themselves in competence, in the knowledge that they could help in return on another occasion. He found that for some individuals the cost of acknowledging inferiority was too great and they therefore avoided seeking advice and help.

Although these observations were made in offices rather than schools, I would suggest they are pertinent in a consideration of social relationships between support teachers and class teachers. As Smith (1982) maintains, '...teachers cannot be effective consultants if a superior or didactic manner deters colleagues from seeking their help...' My experience suggests that an appropriate image for a support teacher is of a friendly colleague, equal in status and competence but holding a particular specialist brief. There is a long tradition of special responsibilities in secondary schools and teachers in primary schools are now often required to act as consultants or advisers to colleagues for an area of the curriculum. This image should help to cultivate relationships characterized by cooperative working and problem sharing.

Observing a particularly skilful support teacher seeking help from colleagues emphasized to me the subtlety and sensitivity which may be required to avoid producing feelings of inferiority or resentment on the part of the class teacher. Rather than *avoiding* situations where they may be seen to be less competent than class teachers, perhaps support teachers should actively *seek them out*, so they can *receive* help and advice which they would then be in a position to reciprocate. This is more difficult for support teachers not attached to schools. A further disadvantage for peripatetic support teachers is that they may not have many opportunities to take part in staffroom conversations which can sometimes be 'consultations in disguise' (Blau op.cit., p. 102). They also miss out on the other social and professional benefits of close links with members of a school staff.

Where should support teachers be based?
Support teachers based in schools have the opportunity to be class teachers for part of the week, which may help establish their credi-

bility with colleagues. There is also less likelihood of their being treated with the suspicion often reserved for 'outside experts'. However, a peripatetic service housed in a central base has two principal advantages. First, not being based full-time in a single school and not being responsible to the senior management of a school may enable support teachers to take a more objective and critical view of the curriculum and organization of schools. Secondly, sharing a central base with colleagues doing a similar job provides opportunities for mutual support and common professional training at both formal and informal levels. Of course, the paradox is that their more objective and critical stance and enhanced skills and knowledge are probably less useful because they are not in as good a position to develop effective problem-sharing relationships!

The experience of assisting in the establishment and reorganization of support services in two LEA's and my knowledge of developments in other authorities has led me to favour the option of school-based services where practicable. This option would seem to be particularly advantageous for services which support the large group of children who experience difficulties of learning and behaviour. Perhaps one disadvantage of being school-based could be overcome if support teachers had a base in one school, but also worked in a number of other schools. If these services are to be school-based, an examination of the role of any existing support teacher(s) and (in secondary schools) of the pastoral system is required.

In the case of the smaller services for children with physical and sensory difficulties, the situation is less clear and the responsibilities of these support teachers usually extend over a much wider geographical area and include a much greater number of schools. However, in principle there is no reason why these support teachers should not also benefit from being based in primary and secondary schools.

There is considerable variation between LEAs in the location and management of teacher support services. In recent months I have been made aware of the following arrangements amongst a small number of LEAs:

- support teachers based in schools responsible to the Adviser (SEN) and AEO (SEN);
- support teachers based in schools and responsible to the head-teachers of these schools;

- support teachers based in schools and responsible to the head teachers of the schools and the Adviser (SEN) or AEO (SEN);
- support teachers in a central base responsible to the Adviser (SEN), AEO (SEN) or Principal Educational Psychologist (PEP), sometimes through a head of service.

In most LEAs, other support services (such as educational social work and educational psychology) are based centrally. Would the interests of children be better served if these services were also school based? Despite the inevitably strong resistance to this suggestion, I would hope that the issue could be discussed openly with an honest recognition of the professional interests which may be helping to stifle such developments.

Accountability and evaluation
Any discussion of the location of support services raises the issues of accountability and evaluation. Many of us can claim to know a support teacher whom we feel is very effective. What criteria are we using to judge effectiveness? One might suggest that some LEAs, quite reasonably, choose to judge support services by their effectiveness in reducing the numbers of requests for formal assessment and placements in special schools. Of course, Goodwin (1983) found that in one LEA with a policy of integration, the development of support services coincided with an increase in the proportion of the school population attending special schools!

Using only the criterion of 'teacher satisfaction with the services' to evaluate their work may seriously undermine the work of support staff in encouraging schools to question their curriculum and organization. It could be argued that doing what senior management and class teachers want support teachers to do may not always be in the best interests of children with special educational needs. I would suggest that any evaluation of the work of support teachers should take account of a number of different perspectives. It would be important to obtain the views of:

- the governors and senior management of the school(s);
- the class teachers who receive support;
- the parents of children who receive support;
- the children who receive support;
- the general or pastoral advisers, Adviser (SEN) and the educational psychologists to the schools concerned;

- the AEO (SEN) and other assistant education officers for schools and colleges.

The issue of accountability seems to me to be inextricably linked with the location of services. Whilst all teachers are accountable to the children they teach and their families, as well as the wider community, there is also a need for them to be accountable on a day-to-day basis to a person or group of people who can oversee their work. If support teachers are based in schools, then I believe they should be accountable for the quality of their work to the head teachers of those schools. Presumably the schools' advisers, and perhaps the special needs adviser, would check periodically that the head was undertaking this responsibility or had delegated the task to a senior member of staff.

Centre-based staff are usually accountable to a head of service or team leader and in some cases to an adviser, principal educational psychologist or assistant education officer. I would suggest that in most LEAs neither advisers, PEPs or assistant education officers have sufficient time to manage a support service. Even if they are relieved of some of their other responsibilities, it is difficult to see how they can have day-to-day contact with support staff. A team leader or head of service is the most obvious alternative solution and increasingly the one being chosen by LEAs. An advantage of this management structure is that support teachers are accountable to a person who is presumably qualified and experienced in the type of work they undertake. The principal disadvantage is that the support of children with SEN and their teachers is made more special and different by this separate management structure and this helps maintain the unfortunate distinction between children who have SEN and those who don't. In addition it helps to 'distance' support services from schools and encourages the development of professional 'empires'.

Concluding Remarks

There can be no doubt that class teachers will continue to need the advice and support of both specialist teachers and colleagues from other caring professions. Discussion of the variations in philosophy, management, organization and practices of these support services can sometimes obscure rather than answer the fundamental question of 'How best can we support children experiencing difficulties in school?' The most important element of this support is the regular class teacher. Interventions by support services must not devalue the major contribution made by class teachers to the support of children with SEN. I am concerned to ensure that support is seen as a two-way process. In both teacher and non-teacher support services we must encourage genuine partnership and problem-sharing with class teachers. To achieve this, we need to make a critical examination of the underlying assumptions, management and practice of support work. This examination must take account of professional interests and social processes in schools.

Chapter 6
The Changing Role of the Educational Psychologist

Gary Thomas

Since Sir Cyril Burt established educational psychology as a profession in the United Kingdom at the beginning of the twentieth century, it has been assuming an ever more important role in the education service. There are now around 1600 educational psychologists in post. They occupy a key place in the assessment of children who are experiencing difficulty at school, and in offering advice both to schools and to LEAs on ways of meeting children's special needs.

But it is doubtful if Sir Cyril, the inventor of schools' psychological services, would recognize as 'educational psychology' many of the activities undertaken by a forward-looking schools' psychological service in the late 1980s. When he became the first educational psychologist in 1911, he set the pattern for decades to follow. The pattern he established was one of ascertainment: until the 1970s the role of the educational psychologist could have been summed up by the term 'test-basher'.

It is unfortunate that such an image should have come to surround the work of the educational psychologist. Educational psychologists who wish to work in a more imaginative way now find it difficult to break free from its chains. Indeed, many expectations restrict and constrain the educational psychologist who wishes to work in non-traditional ways. What are these expectations, and how have they developed?

Educational Psychologists: their expected Role

From their beginnings, schools' psychological services have been concerned with ascertainment. An educational system which segregated out those who couldn't (or wouldn't) fit, needed tools and people to do the job of segregation. Tests and educational psychologists fitted the bill admirably. Educational psychologists' background in academic psychology gave them skills in test construction and administration, and their experience in teaching was valuable in putting the test scores into context. The profession developed: the need of the educational system for more and better ascertainment in times when problems in schools seemed to be growing, resulted in more and more educational psychologists being employed. As seems inevitable in the growth of any new profession, all the trappings of professionalism came to accompany this process. Thus, educational psychologists formed their own professional organization, the *Association of Educational Psychologists*, which monitors entry standards into the profession. Educational psychologists are required to have a good honours degree in psychology, at least two years' teaching experience, and a postgraduate qualification in educational psychology – usually a master's degree.

As all this happened – as the professional crystallized and practices were reinforced by a variety of legal requirements on local education authorities – so attitudes about the role of the educational psychologist became clearer in mind of the teaching profession: the educational psychologist was the tester. Many a newly-trained educational psychologist has gone into a school for the first time and been ushered into the medical room or empty classroom to do tests almost before having the chance to mutter 'Classroom observation?'.

Alongside the growth of the profession – indeed stimulating its growth between the 1930s and the post-war period – was the growth in the child guidance service. Child guidance services flourished at a time when psychiatry and psychoanalysis enjoyed a novelty interest in society generally. Interest in the writings of Freud, Jung and Adler was high. The concept of child guidance, conceived on the other side of the Atlantic and comprising as it did a multiprofessional assessment and diagnosis, was new, attractive and credible. Indeed for many workers in child guidance, the idea was a 'dream' (Sampson, 1975). The multiprofessional team comprised a psychiatrist, a psychologist and a social worker. Typically, the educational psychologist would assess the child using tests, the social worker would make a detailed family history and the psychiatrist would see the child. Then, under the doctor's direction, the team would meet to discuss the diagnosis and treatment plan. The set-up seemed eminently sensible and the clinics burgeoned. The growing profession of educational psychology shared in this success.

These developments meant that teachers came to see educational psychologists as people who worked for most of their time in child guidance clinics and occasionally visited schools. Wherever they did their work, they used tests.

The changes of the last 20 years

It would be over-dramatic to claim that this picture – a picture of a young profession confident in its role and optimistic about its steady growth in the post-war period – has cracked. Indeed the 1981 Act has provided a new stimulus to the employment of educational psychologists. Nevertheless, there has been a sustained period of self-questioning and self-doubt about practices which had become the shibboleths of the profession. Self-consciousness about, for instance, the use of tests is summarized in the titles of articles written at the beginning of the 1970s – titles like 'If we throw tests out of the window what else is there left to do?' Burden (1973); many educational psychologists were beginning to feel that tests were to psychologists as new clothes were to emperors. And doubts about the success of the multidisciplinary teamwork approach of child guidance were beginning to emerge. It seemed that testing and multiprofessional teamwork, the twin pillars upon which the growth of the profession had rested, were beginning to crack.

But all was not gloom and despair. At the end of the 1970s a compilation entitled *Reconstructing Educational Psychologist* (Gillham, 1978) was published. Containing chapters about community psychology, systems work in schools (in other words seeing the *school system* as the client rather than the *individual child*) and the end of psychometrics, it perhaps summarized the optimism and liberal-mindedness of two decades. It foresaw a widening role for the educational psychologist. Indeed, the last 20 years have seen quite substantial changes take place in the work of the educational psychologist for a number of reasons...

Reasons for change

1. *Integration*

There has been a reappraisal of the way that the education system deals with children with disabilities or children who have some other kind of difficulty at school. This has been marked by the Warnock Report and the 1981 Act. Moves to integration mean that ascertainment in the traditional sense, with precise quasi-scientific advice on children's placement, is less frequently required.

In times gone by, the psychologist was the purveyor of 'objective' information obtained from *standardized* tests. The educational psychologist was the disinterested party from outside who would make a judgement, based on these tests, about the future of the child. Because the educational psychologist's tests had been standardized on large numbers of children, there was no danger (the argument went) that unfair judgements would be made of children's abilities. The test, administered by the educational psychologists, would be the final arbiter of a child's suitability for a particular kind of school. The reasons for the use of tests lie in the history of special education. Tests were designed and used in an education system whose architects assumed that it would be to every child's benefit if children who did not fit were educated separately. Tests were the fairest and most efficient way of selecting those children, and psychologists, as the inventors of psychometric tests, were the most appropriate people to be administering them.

It is now recognized that there is far more to meeting children's needs than simply categorizing them (for instance via an IQ figure) and then placing them in a school of the appropriate category. The changes in thinking about disability, handicap and special needs which were articulated in the Warnock Report have encouraged educational psychologists, teachers and others involved in children's education to meet children's needs in the mainstream. As this becomes more commonplace, the ascertainment function of the educational psychologist is increasingly becoming redundant.

Inevitably, the response to an ascertainment was either satisfaction that the child would be moving to a special school where s/he would be receiving an appropriate education, or dissatisfaction with the fact that the teacher would have to battle on, trying to teach the child in the ordinary school with no extra help provided. The classroom teacher's frustration at the latter encapsulated what was wrong with the educational psychologist's response: it was about ascertainment rather than assessment. The tests which the educational psychologist used served what was really an administrative function – not one which was educational. As, increasingly, referral to the educational psychologist constituted a request for help and advice in the mainstream classroom setting, the irrelevance of the traditional tests became increasingly manifest. This point merits a further look...

2. *Dissatisfaction with tests*

There has been a growing dissatisfaction with psychometric tests – the traditional tools of the trade of the educational psychologist. Both psychologists and teachers have been critical of the way in which tests provide very little useful information to the teacher. Often the tests are criticized as merely telling the teacher what he or she already knows. If they were not providing ascertainment for special school, tests could do little more than confirm that the child had a problem, but one which was not so serious that transfer to special school was merited. Teachers did not want the educational psychologist to confirm that the child had a problem – they knew that, or they wouldn't have referred the child in the first place.

The design and widespread use of psychometric tests rested on the assumption that mental abilities remained fairly stable over time, and that they could be reliably measured. This assumption is now far less widely held. Indeed, the notion that there is some general, measurable 'ability factor', which can be used as the basis for prognoses about the child has lost credibility among most educational psychologists. Tests tell you what you knew already – usually that the child isn't doing very well at school. IQ tests, even the best parts of the best IQ tests, are no better at predicting a child's performance in two, three or four years, than are simple reading tests.

The failure of traditional tests not only to provide any useful information on *teaching* the child, but also to elicit any information on the *future performance* of the child, led to the development of a new breed of *diagnostic* tests like the *ITPA* (the *Illinois Test of Psycholinguistic Abilities*). The assumption was that with the diagnosis of the child's strengths and weaknesses that the test made, it would be possible to devise a remediation programme which would help solve the child's problems. Tests like this were good news for educational psychologists wedded to the traditional mould. Here were tests which gave them some reason for existing again. But unfortunately things were not to be that easy – as is usually the case in education. As soon as evaluations of these diagnoses and remedial programmes were made, it became clear that they were no more effective than any other kind of treatment (see, for example, Newcomer and Hammill, 1975). In fact, it seemed that sometimes children in receipt of this kind of 'help' would ultimately do less well than children who simply received drill in reading.

The uncomfortable lesson for educational psychologists and teachers was that via tests there appeared to be no way of quickly getting to the root of a child's problem and then suggesting strategies for overcoming it.

3. *Discontent with the traditional model of child guidance*
The way in which child guidance clinics work has come under scrutiny. Research indicates that child guidance clinics have long waiting lists, only scratch at the surface of the number of problems that exist and ultimately do not have much effect on the children they work with (see Tizard, 1973, for a fuller discussion). The multi-professional ideal behind the services has proved consistently difficult to realize in practice, resulting in a DES recommendation (in DES Circular 3/74) that 'networks' of services should operate, instead of teams of different professionals. As a result, the tendency has been for schools' psychological services to split away from child guidance clinics. Now, the organizations are often housed in separate premises and often they are responsible to different heads, with the schools' psychologist, and the Child Guidance Clinic perhaps responsible to a consultant psychiatrist.

Even where child guidance clinics and schools' psychological services have remained under the same roof and the same head, it is probably fair to say that most educational psychologists separate (in their minds, if nowhere else) their schools' psychological service work from their child guidance clinic work. The former will probably occupy most of their time and will involve a great deal of work in schools. The educational psychologist is only likely to refer on to a psychiatrist or child guidance social worker if there is some particularly difficult or unusual problem in which it is felt that the support and guidance of other professionals would be valuable.

4. A realization that psychology has more to offer education than simply testing

There has been a growing recognition that psychology is concerned with more than simply testing, and that trained educational psychologists have more to offer schools, teachers, parents and children than they had traditionally been offering. In industry advice is sought from psychologists on management, the working of groups, work design, the presentation of images, the readability of text, the surveying of attitudes and a host of other diverse topics. But thinking in the education system seems to have been constrained until very recently by the traditional expectations of the educational psycholgist.

More recently, though, and especially as the failings of psychometrics have become more obvious, educational psychologists have begun to seek out alternative applications of psychology to education. The manifest relevance of behavioural psychology to real life problems has, for instance, spawned a host of techniques and applications which collectively go under the name of 'behaviour modification'. Educational psychologists may run workshops for teachers on managing stress, or they may help to set up, organize and run support groups for parents of children with special needs. The applications of the various branches of psychology to education are almost limitless, yet it is only recently that they have been explored in a less inhibited way.

5. Changes in in-service education for teachers

Recently there have been profound changes in the way that in-service education for teachers has been funded. There is far more 'in-house', in-service education being provided in schools, and already there are far more calls on educational psychologists to contribute to, or organize, aspects of this INSET. These changes will see the consolidation and enhancement of a trend which was already occurring, with educational psychologists doing more preventive and consultative work in schools.

6. The importance of educational psychologists in the education system

There has been a consolidation of the place of the educational psychologist in the education system. The Summerfield Report of 1968 (Summerfield, 1968) examined the way in which educational psychologists work and made a number of recommendations, most significantly about the ratio of educational psychologists to school children. In 1975 a DES circular (GB.DES, 1975) introduced new procedures which made it the responsibility of the educational psychologist, rather than the school medical officer, to make a recommendation to the local education authority about provision for children thought to be in need of special education. And most significantly, the 1981 Education Act placed a statutory obligation on local education authorities to obtain an assessment from an educational psychologist about such children.

All this has meant that psychologists now occupy an important place in the education system and they are often involved in planning developments in that service, or in evaluating existing structures.

However, many would claim that new procedures, especially those instituted after the 1981 Act, have been something of a mixed blessing. While the procedures were introduced with the best of motives (rationalizing assessment and ensuring the involvement of parents at every stage), in practice they have often involved the educational psychologist in far more purely administrative work. They have pushed the centre of gravity of educational psychologists' work away from schools, parents and children toward educational administration.

The changes in practice

How have these changes made themselves felt in practice? The question can perhaps be answered by looking at the work of an imaginary educational psychologist in 1967 and 1987. In 1967, before the Summerfield Report (which recommended that there should be a ratio of one educational psychologist to every 10,000 schoolchildren), the educational psychologist would have had to serve dozens of schools and could quite possibly have been responsible for double the number of children recommended by Summerfield. If the psychologist worked in a child guidance clinic he or she may have been working under the medical direction of a child psychiatrist who may even have given specific directions on the kinds of tests the educational psychologist was to do. Though the educational psychologist would make visits to schools, these would represent something of a special occasion, and usually children would be invited to the clinic for their appointments, whether the problem was felt in the home or the school. Irrespective of the problem, the psychologist's response would be heavily dependent upon the use of tests, usually incorporating some kind of ability testing.

By 1987, our imaginary educational psychologist would, almost certainly, have had the opportunity to work in a very different way. He or she would be responsible to a smaller group of schools, and may have been lucky enough to work in one of the local authorities enlightened enough to have met the Warnock Report's recommendation that LEAs should provide one educational psychologist for every 5,000 children. Although justifiably bemoaning the fact that the 1981 Act gave educational psychologists a great deal more administrative work to undertake, they would nevertheless probably be doing considerably more than testing. They are likely to be involved in schools in a number of ways: they may be working far more in the classroom alongside the class teacher; they may be doing in-service work with teachers, or undertaking preventative or consultative work in schools; they may be working as specialists in a particular area, or perhaps working very closely with parents. Each of these merits some closer attention.

• **Working in the classroom**, perhaps working with children in that context, in order to help the teacher develop ways of tackling children's learning difficulties. Much of the criticism of the educational psychologist's traditional *modus operandi* is centred around his or her insularity from the 'real world'. Bronfenbrenner (1979) has criticized the whole approach of developmental and child psychology as the study of the *strange* behaviour of children in *strange* situations with *strange* adults. Such a criticism can aptly be applied to the work of the educational psychologist as it used to be undertaken. The move of today's educational psychologist into the classroom reflects a sensitivity to this criticism.

• **Providing in-service work in the school**, perhaps using one of the many 'packages' which have been devised for this purpose. Now that far more in-service work is being undertaken in schools, and schools have their own budgets of in-service education, they are calling far more on support services to contribute to these programmes of advanced education. While educational psychologists at some times will respond to such a demand by devising their own courses, lectures or workshops, at other times they will make use of a marketed 'package' developed with this purpose in mind.

One of the first such packages was *EDY* (*Education of the Developmentally Young*) (McBrien and Foxen, 1981). *EDY* was devised for use by educational psychologists or advisers with teachers in schools for children with severe learning difficulties. Through study texts, video demonstration, and guided practice with children, the educational psychologist takes the trainee (usually a teacher, nursery nurse or ancillary helper) through the elements of a structured approach to working with such children.

• **Consulting with teachers**, perhaps after having allocated a specific amount of time to the school. Such an approach has come to be known as 'time-contracting'. Such contracting of time was seen initially as a way of responding to the enormous demands on the educational psychologist's time. Educational psychologists had to find a way of sharing their time fairly among the various schools for which they were responsible. Some schools – and not necessarily those with the most serious problems – would refer large numbers of children. Many educational psychologists found that the distribution of their time was being dictated not by 'need', but by the assertiveness of the head teachers in the schools on their patches. Time-contracting developed as a way of getting around such a problem, and it is now widely used. The system simply involves educational psychologists allocating a specific amount of time to each school on their patch, and saying to the school 'This is the time I can give you – you are free to use it in the way you see best'. Thus, after negotiation with the educational psychologist, the head of a small infant school may contract with the educational psychologist to receive half a day a term, while a large comprehensive school or a special school may be visited once a fortnight. Under this system, the school has to make decisions about the use of this time. A single intensive assessment by the educational psychologist – involving perhaps observation, assessment, discussion with parents and teacher – may take all morning and thus consume all the time allocated to the school for the term. Faced with this, the school may well decide that a problem is not serious enough to warrant such intervention. The head and staff may respond by asking the educational psychologist to use the contracted time to join a meeting with the teachers in the school to discuss children about whom general concern is felt, or to discuss wider issues such as behaviour management or assessment. Of course, there has to be flexibility in the use of a system like this; it is not uncommon for a school suddenly, and for no apparent reason, to find itself faced with a number of children about whom serious concern is felt. It is the statutory responsibility of the educational psychologist to make an assessment of such children.

• **Specializing in a particular area of work**, such as work with pre-school children. There has been a recognition in some schools' psychological services that individual educational psychologists cannot each carry the expertise adequately to cope with the wide range of problems which children might experience. The problem is felt in particular in areas where – because, mercifully, the incidence of the disability is very low (as for example autism or visual handicap) – educational psychologists may only very rarely come across affected children. In such circumstances, educational psychologists may be unable to develop or maintain the skills of knowledge of work satisfactorily with such children and their families. In many services, specialisms develop out of the educational psychologists' association with particular schools; for instance, an educational psychologist may have in his or her 'patch' a school for children with hearing impairment, and may develop an expertise with such children. Or, because of an educational psychologist's interest in a particular area, negotiation with colleagues may result in their taking on responsibility for that area of work. These individuals may then come to be used as consultants by their colleagues.

• **Working closely with parents**. The educational psychologist may, for example, be working with a school on a scheme of paired-reading, helping the school to assist parents who wish to become more involved in their children's education. In some schools' psychological services, work with the parents of pre-school handicapped children has become highly developed; using the *Portage Early Education Programme* (Bluma *et al.*, 1987) parents have been taught how to develop and enhance the abilities of their children. Such work has usually been very well received.

Conclusion

The support offered by the educational psychologist has broadened in many ways, but this broadening has not occurred at the pace that many would have expected or wished. Moves to a more liberal view of the education system generally have been halted by the *zeitgeist* of the 1980s. The public services, including education, have been afforded a lower priority since the beginning of the decade. Now, the talk is not of the limited utility of testing, but of an *increase* in testing, not just for children who may be experiencing difficulty, but for all children at the ages of seven, 11, 14 and 16. The curriculum is being seen once again as a series of subjects about which children should learn. In this climate it would be extraordinary if there were no ripples felt in the educational psychologist's work.

But even if there cannot be many grounds for optimism on this score, educational psychologists can be content with the transformation which has taken place in the service they offer to their consumers. Both the growth in psychology and fundamental changes in education have been reflected in the development of educational psychology over this century. The maturation of the profession has been accompanied by a desire among educational psychologists to seek alternative and better ways of supporting teacher colleagues. The increased self-confidence of the educational psychologist in seeking out and using such alternatives has been facilitated, or perhaps enabled, by a changing perception of the educational psychologist on the part of the consumer – teacher, parent or child. No longer is the educational psychologist seen as the test-basher or even the trouble-shooter. Rather, psychologists are seen as colleagues with whom work can be undertaken collaboratively to better the education service provided for all children.

Chapter 7
The Role of the Psychiatric Social Worker

Howard Williams

Family and child guidance clinics have existed in the United Kingdom for nearly 50 years. They were developed as a specialized response for helping children who were causing serious concern to parents, schools or doctors because of problems in their emotional or social development, their behaviour or learning. The age-range of children referred to a clinic was from about three years to the mid-teens.

Traditionally there was a basic 'medical model' of individual intrapsychic disturbance, which took primacy over unsatisfactory interpersonal relationships as the focus for professional attention – though of course the latter were recognized as relevant to the child's problems. The work of the clinics took place within a psychoanalytic theoretical framework as a way of understanding the nature of the child's problems and for informing the treatment of the child.

The professional training of a psychiatric social worker (PSW) includes experience of working in a psychiatric setting, such as a psychiatric unit for children or adolescents or in an adult psychiatric clinic or hospital. This training prepares the psychiatric social worker for understanding family relationships and the significant disturbances in these relationships which can predispose a child to emotional, behavioural and learning problems within the family, at school and in wider society.

The traditional practice model for family and child guidance clinics in the United Kingdom has been the multidisciplinary team, comprising child psychiatrist, educational psychologist, psychiatric social worker and, in some clinics, a child psychotherapist (who would work exclusively with selected, individual children). The team members would come together, for the purpose of their joint work, to a specified clinic location: for most this is a community-based rather than a hospital-based clinic, though it can include the latter.

Each team member's role has a specific focus and function. Team leadership almost invariably devolved onto the psychiatrist who, as well as the child psychotherapist, would undertake the direct treatment of the referred child in the context of relationships in the family, school and wider social life.

Until the early 1970s, the psychiatric social worker's functions were primarily threefold:

- sensitive interviewing of the child's parents in gathering information regarding family relationships and social factors, to enable the clinic team to formulate a treatment plan;
- emotional support and counselling for the child's parents;
- liaison with school, primary health care workers (family doctors and health visitors) and with other relevant social agencies.

Occasionally, the psychiatric social worker might work directly with a child if the clinic team thought this to be appropriate.

Recent Developments

In the early 1970s, a number of developments had begun to occur in the USA and the United Kingdom which led to significant changes in the theoretical framework for thinking about and dealing with the child and family problems which were referred to clinics. Very briefly these developments can be described under the broad heading of a systems approach, which emphasized patterns of interaction and communication between all members *within* a social system, such as a family, and between a system and *other* systems within the wider environment.

These relatively recent developments have led to changes in professional roles and in professional practice in the emergence of family therapy with its emphasis on the family as a constantly interacting group with specific developmental tasks which need to be dealt with adequately at the time they arise in the life-cycle of the family.

During the past 15 years there has been a burgeoning of family therapy theory and practice which has given attention to the nuclear and extended family within their culture and over several generations. It has highlighted specific aspects of family life such as family structure, patterns of interaction and communication between family members, roles, rules governing behaviour, boundaries between the generations and genders, belief systems, family myths and the coping skills and strengths of the family.

What these changes have meant for the psychiatric social worker's role is that it is now expected that, either alone or with a clinical colleague, he or she assesses the significance to a family of a referral problem and, using a professional understanding of family functioning, makes specific interventions in clinic meetings with the family. The interventions made by the psychiatric social worker (either when working solo or in partnership with a child psychiatrist or educational psychologist) have the aim of trying to induce change in family relationships that will relieve distress, achieve a good-enough resolution of the referred problem and also promote within the family or school more satisfactory ways of handling the referred child.

So, briefly, the role of the psychiatric social worker has widened to include direct interventions with the whole family group or with the marital/parental couple or with the individual child, whichever focus seems most appropriate, as well as offering consultative advice on ways of handling the child at home, in school and in specialized settings such as children's homes and hostels.

Operation of Family and Child Guidance Clinics

In the majority of clinics, there is a system of 'open referral' which means that whenever there is valid concern regarding a child's behaviour, learning, emotional or social development, then that child can be referred to a clinic – with the knowledge and consent of the parents – by a professional worker such as teacher, school counsellor, education social worker, family doctor, health visitor, social services department, probation officer, hospital, voluntary organization or by the family themselves contacting the clinic.

In practice, the youngest children referred tend to be around three years old and the eldest around 16 years. Occasionally teenagers will refer themselves without parental knowledge and requesting that their parents are not informed. This type of situation raises particular aspects of confidentiality and of ways of working creatively with 'secret' information.

The psychiatric social workers in a clinic are responsible for dealing with all referrals from a defined geographical area. The problems referred to a clinic vary according to the age of the child. The range includes:

- behaviour problems at home and at school;
- aggressive, persistent attention-seeking or disruptive behaviour;
- age-inappropriate bed-wetting, soiling, sleep disturbances;
- emotional disturbance manifesting in social withdrawal, apathy, excessive timidity, chronic sadness, depression, recurring relationship problems, social isolation;
- children with chronic learning difficulties who are performing significantly below their level of ability;
- school refusers and truanting children;
- children with delays in their emotional and social development.

Many of the children referred for help are from families disrupted by parental separation, divorce or death or where the two-parent family has never been established. An increasing number of children referred are from 'reconstituted' step-families, and approximately twice as many boys are referred compared with the number of girls.

The following case studies serve to illustrate the kind of referrals made to the family and child guidance clinic and the kind of progress that can be subsequently achieved:

Case example: Edward (aged three)

Edward lived with his parents and younger brother. He was referred by the family doctor because of aggression towards other children in the playgroup and frequent temper tantrums at home, when he would attack his brother. Edward was a bright, energetic and healthy child. One playgroup had excluded him because of his behaviour, but the present playgroup was containing him. Mother, who bore the brunt of his behaviour, seemed exhausted and exasperated.

The whole family were seen at the clinic by the child psychiatrist and a psychiatric social worker as co-therapists. It became apparent that Edward responded well to father's warm, firm handling and clear messages, which contrasted with his poor response to mother's negative injunctions, her anxious expectancy that he would misbehave and hurt his brother and her seemingly depressed state of mind. Mother worked part-time and at week-ends father took over the care of both children.

Work with the family focused on

- helping the parents to develop a more positive, consistent framework for Edward including specific strategies for handling him;
- enabling mother to express strongly-felt frustrations and resentments about her childhood and her present life;
- assistance from the health visitor and financial help from the education and social services departments;
- an experienced mother of grown-up children was recruited to the playgroup to give Edward one-to-one support.

This special worker and Edward's mother trusted each other, so that mother felt able to share his care some afternoons each week, giving her and Edward planned respites from each other. This shared caring increased Edward's positive experiences with adults and it reduced the pressures on mother. Clinic contact with the parents continued, enabling them to understand more about their own relationship and their attitudes to their children. It was possible to set in motion a more benign cycle of interaction between Edward and his mother and consequently a more effective socialization in preparation for his entering primary school.

Case example: Anthony (aged 15)

Anthony was referred by this school because of minor truanting and poor academic progress over the previous year, although he was well above average intelligence. He lived with his parents and sister aged 13. The whole family were seen at the clinic by the psychiatric social worker and the educational psychologist who worked as co-therapists.

It emerged during the first meeting with the family that the parents were planning to separate as a first step to divorce. The children had not been told explicitly about this but intuitively they expected it. Direct communication between the parents was minimal and the children were in the roles of 'go-between' for their parents. The family seemed divided into two camps, with Anthony closer to his mother and his sister close to father. The distress in the family was clearly articulated by both children who wished their parents to stay together.

Although the marital relationship had broken down, both parents were devoted to their children. There had developed a pattern of confused responsibilities in which Anthony – and to a lesser extent his sister – had assumed responsibility for attempting to keep his parents together whilst the parents felt themselves responsible for the quality of his school work.

These issues were explored during four meetings with the family which extended over a few months. Communication between the parents was improved; this probably was connected with it being made clear to the parents at the outset that the therapists were not attempting marital reconciliation. The parents together made their position clear to the children and helped to release Anthony from his role of 'marriage broker'. He began to take more interest in his studies and gained his qualifications. The parents separated and involved both children appropriately in their arrangements for regular access.

Consultation

An important aspect of the psychiatric social worker's role is that of being accessible to other professionals in education, health and social welfare agencies for consultation regarding concern about a child's difficulties at home, school or in other contexts. This availability applies also to families who may wish to write, telephone or call into a clinic to discuss their concern about a child.

In many instances, this informal consultation will remove the necessity for an explicit referral of a child, for, as frequently happens, clarification of ideas leads to the emergence of new ways of responding to the problematic situation; this enables the concerned adult to act more confidently and effectively. However, more often, this process of consultation will clarify the situation sufficiently to enable the professional worker or parent to make an explicit referral of the child to a clinic. The following example helps to illustrate the process of consultation and how it can lead to effective and appropriate action:

Case example: Julie (aged six)

Julie lived with her mother and two younger brothers. Her parents were divorced and she had no contact with her father, who had looked after her for most of her first two years when mother had temporarily deserted. There was a problem of 'bonding' between Julie and her mother, who nevertheless wished to do her best for her.

The special needs teacher referred Julie. At school she seemed to 'ebb and flow' in her responsiveness – sometimes alert and at other times described as 'far away and day-dreaming'. She seemed to have hardly any idea of a work task and she used the one-to-one contact with the special needs teacher to form a dependent relationship and little else. Progress in acquisitional learning was negligible.

In liaison with the educational psychologist and school, Julie was given additional special provision in small group and one-to-one contexts and mother was encouraged to visit school on a regular basis to see her work and progress.

The child psychiatrist and the psychiatric social worker saw mother and the three children at the clinic to explore ways of improving the relationship between mother and Julie, who was seen by mother as 'Daddy's girl'. Efforts to revive father's contact with his children failed. Clinic contact with the family and liaison with the school lasted for about a year. Mother formed a cautious new relationship with a single man who appeared well-disposed towards all three children at the clinic and he came to several of the family meetings. Mother was able to review aspects of her own childhood, which helped her in her relationship with Julie and her two sons. Mother reported that she was getting more enjoyment with Julie. At school, Julie had begun to make progress.

The Process of Referral of a Child to Family and Child Guidance Clinic

Following the initial consultation with the psychiatric social worker, and where a decision has been made to refer a child, the psychiatric social worker sends to the professional worker concerned a clinic referral form for the referrer to complete, and also a form for the parent(s) to complete. If parents are referring their own child then one form is sent, and only to them. Occasionally, parents will refuse to complete a referral form or do not do so because of a seeming inability to focus conceptually on the questions contained in the form. Both of these responses in themselves offer some information about the family on which to base initial work by the psychiatric social worker with the family.

Clinic referral form

The aim of the referral form is to clarify and specify the *nature* of the problem as seen by the referring person(s) and also what has been done to *deal* with it. Essentially, the same questions are contained in the form sent to a professional referrer and in the one sent to the parents. There are six questions:

- how would you describe the situation?
- how has the situation been handled up to now?
- what has been the outcome so far?
- what changes do you want first?
- why is our help being asked for at this time?
- is there any other information you wish to give?

The referring person is asked to be as specific as possible in completing the form, so that there can be a clear focus on what is agreed to be the problem and on the best use that can be made of the time spent with the child and the family.

In the great majority of referrals, there is a workable consensus between all concerned adults regarding what constitutes the presenting problem. However, in some cases the parents may not agree between themselves in their definitions of the situation and some families may request one form for each parent to express their different views. In other cases, a school's perception of a child will differ substantially from that of the parents.

Where such discrepancies of view exist, these have to be resolved and a consensus agreed upon at the outset of any systemic work with the family/school/other professionals, for any effective intervention to be possible. School-based clinics, where the child and the family meet simultaneously with the psychiatric social worker, educational psychologist and the appropriate member of school staff, seem to afford a good practice model for dealing economically with any serious discrepancy between the perceptions of school and family. Such discrepancies may be utilized as part of the intervention to induce change.

Additionally it helps the clinic to have information regarding *previous* referrals of the child, when and to whom he or she was referred; also it is important to know if the family is currently in active contact with any other professional helping agency, so that unnecessary confusions can be avoided.

The process of sending the clinic referral form and reqesting the family and the referring agent to think about the current predicament in response to structured questions, is in itself an intervention in starting to induce change in the interactional system of the child and the family. Frequently, parents will describe how, in completing the form, they had discussed their perceptions of the situation in a fresh way that has offered a prospect of beginning to move the 'log-jam' in a positive direction.

As in all work with interactional problems, it is necessary to be as specific and unambiguous as possible, so that clear operational goals can be established with the child and the family. Sometimes the parents, or a school, when completing the referral form, will note that in terms of desired changes they wish the child 'to be more positive' or 'show more self-confidence' or 'to show more respect' or 'to be happy' or 'to get on better with peers' or 'to enjoy life more'. When the psychiatric social worker meets the person who has requested these unspecific changes, it is necessary to negotiate an agreed bench-mark in asking them for a 'video description' of what, in their view, the child would specifically need to do, need to look like, need to sound like if he became 'more positive', 'more self-confident', 'more respectful', 'happier' and so on. It is then possible to agree realistic operational goals with the family or school in ways that are appropriate to that particular case.

A psychiatric social worker works with the avowed aim of

promoting change in the referred child's network of relationships, because the central message of every referral is 'help to change this situation' in some specified or unspecified way. The therapeutic work takes place in a context where a psychiatric social worker and a co-therapist need to understand their part in the relationship network inside and around each family. The therapists attempt to influence this network and the network influences the therapists, inevitably evoking a wide range of personal feelings. A psychiatric social worker has to create with the family a context which is safe enough for the family to acknowledge and explore aspects of their lives which are frequently intimate, painful and highly-charged. The aim is to move towards a way of handling their problems that will be less distressing than the present situation and will offer them more choice of action. The example of Robert serves to illustrate this:

Case example: Robert (aged six)

Robert was referred by mother because of frequent conflicts between them and his 'defiance' of her. He lived with his divorced mother and two younger brothers. Father was in prison because of serious physical violence to several adults including his wife. Much of the violence had been witnessed by the children.

At school Robert was considered to be of high intelligence, articulate and demanding attention through minor disruptions, unspecific aches and pains and wanting to return home to reassure himself that mother was alright. He was chronically anxious and his work was considerably below his ability level.

Work with mother and child was undertaken jointly by the psychiatric social worker and clinical psychologist and initial interventions aimed at strengthening mother's authority at home. It became apparent that Robert had been so upset by the parental violence that he needed therapeutic time and space on his own. Robert was seen on his own by the psychiatric social worker and through the medium of his drawings, play material and puppets, he re-enacted parts of the disturbing violent events. Strong emotions were expressed by him; these were contained and reviewed with Robert alone and also with him and mother together.

Liaison with school involved supporting his experienced teacher in dealing with his insistent demands for her attention and in encouraging regular school visits by mother to see Robert's work and to discuss him with his teacher. This framework around Robert seemed appropriate because of his insecurities.

Aspects of Clinical Work and Procedures for Handling Cases

Once a child has been referred to the clinic, therapeutic work takes place in;
- a family and child guidance clinic, a health centre or in a specific part of a hospital;
- a school-based clinic (where a child has been referred by the school);
- where appropriate, in the family's home.

It is clearly important to have flexibility of response by the clinic team to any request for help. Such flexibility can lead to one of a number of ways of responding to a request:
- Following a consultation with the psychiatric social worker, the person requesting help (who may be a school teacher, health visitor, social worker or a parent) continues to manage the situation themselves either with or without continuing consultative back-up from the psychiatric social worker.
- Where a request for help has crystallized into an explicit referral of a child to the clinic, then 'face-to-face' work with the whole or part of the child's family is undertaken by the psychiatric social worker alone or in partnership with a child psychiatrist or educational psychologist, in one of the locations mentioned above.

The focus of such 'face-to-face' work can be on:
- the entire family of a referred child (sometimes including grandparents, step-parents and other members of the extended family);
- the child's parents on their own (where it is necessary to be clear whether the focus of work is with them as parents or as marital partners);
- the referred child alone.

Where any of these forms of contact occur in a school-based clinic, the child's year tutor or teacher or a special needs staff member is usually invited to attend the whole meeting, or part of it. This will depend on the specific issues being discussed, on their relevance to the school dimension and on considerations of confidentiality.

Frequency of contact with a referred child and the family varies according to the nature of the problem, the age and needs of the child and the specific form of intervention attempted by the psychiatric social worker. In some instances there is weekly contact during a particular phase of the work or during a crisis. In other cases, the optimum frequency is every few weeks, depending on what changes are taking place and on their significance. Unlike individual psychotherapy, there is no hard and fast rule governing the frequency of clinical contact but there should be a flexibility which takes account of the factors mentioned above. The duration of meetings with a family or child also varies according to the changing needs of the case. It can range from under an hour to around two hours.

When two therapists (for example, a child psychiatrist and psychiatric social worker) are working together in a meeting with a family, they will at the outset negotiate with the family a 'half time' break for consultation, lasting five to ten minutes. This will enable the co-therapists, away from the family, to evaluate what is taking place in the meeting and to clarify the best way of proceeding for the remainder of the meeting. This 'breather' also offers the family an opportunity to reflect on what has been discussed with the therapists.

Case example: Trevor (aged 12)

Trevor lived with mother, stepfather, sister (15) and half-brother (four). His parents divorced when he was six, distressing him deeply. Father had remarried and had young stepdaughters. There had been concern about Trevor in his two primary schools because of poor concentration and memory, poor progress and mood swings. He had received special small-group and one-to-one provision, which had helped his learning. He was assessed as having average intelligence.

Trevor was referred by the senior school and by mother because of disruptive behaviour in class, extreme mood swings at home and at school, also erratic academic progress and having no friends. He visited father fortnightly, sharing his attention with father's step-daughters. Trevor, together with mother and his stepfather, was seen at school by the psychiatric social worker, educational psychologist and year tutor. It became clear that he had considerable power in the family to get mother's anxious attention by his erratic behaviour. Also he seemed extremely angry with all the significant adults in his life and with himself, expressing self-hatred. Mother and stepfather had a good relationship and made great efforts to understand and help Trevor.

Over several meetings with the family, work focused on acknowledging Trevor's distress about his parents' divorce and his belief that he had contributed to it, also on the sense of loss, grief and anger with his parents. This helped him to redefine his expectations of his parents and was linked with the positive elements in his relationship with his stepfather. Further work involved meeting with father and stepmother to consolidate the changes which had helped Trevor in his communication with adults at home and at school, as well as beginning to strengthen his self-esteem.

Further Collaboration with Agencies

In order to understand a child's needs, it is necessary to see that child in context, so that the clinic assessment takes account of family life, school environment and wider social network. In relation to specific aspects of a child's cognitive learning difficulties, the psychiatric social worker needs to liaise with the educational psychologist, class teacher and special needs staff as part of the multiprofessional process.

When a child is being considered for referral to the clinic, it is necessary to first exclude organic or physiological reasons as possible causative factors in the situation. Where appropriate, this medical 'screening' is suggested to the person making a referral, so that the child's family doctor or a medical specialist will examine the child. Once possible physical factors have been excluded, clinical work proceeds on the principle of observing, understanding and handling all phenomena on a systematic basis, that is, as occurring in a constantly interacting system.

Occasionally a referred child and his or her family are currently known to the Social Services department, or the child may already be in care. In these cases, there is consultation with the social worker: where appropriate, the psychiatric social worker and social worker work as co-therapists with the family, either in the family and child guidance clinic, or in the family's home. The psychiatric social worker and the area team social worker jointly assess how a family is functioning and the extent to which the parents are currently and potentially capable of caring for their children. In such joint work, a specified number of meetings would be agreed with the family at the outset and a review of progress would take place with the family at the end of, approximately, four meetings. If necessary, an extended 'contract' is agreed with the family and a further review of the situation would be made, enabling the parents to decide on the best option for the family.

In all instances of this sort of family work, where there are school-age children involved, there is close collaboration with the school and specific ways of supporting the children in school are discussed with the class teacher and special needs staff. Occasionally, where a family with serious problems is known to a number of agencies (school, social services department, family doctor, health visitor, psychiatric social worker), a case conference is convened by the school or by social services department. The various agencies will then make a joint assessment of the situation, sometimes with the parents present for all or part of the meeting, and a joint plan of action can be decided. The following are two examples of collaboration work between the psychiatric social worker and another professional, which enabled progress to be achieved in different circumstances.

Case example: Colin (aged seven)

Colin lived with his parents and his sister (aged four). He was referred jointly by school and parents because of aggressive, defiant and disruptive behaviour at home and at school, where his progress was unsatisfactory. Colin responded better to males than to females and when a firm framework was provided at school as part of a special containment, his concentration improved. He was healthy and of average intelligence; he could understand the concept of a work task and he had friends. In this case, work focused on the parents' inconsistent handling of Colin, which he exploited and which coloured his expectations of how teachers would respond to him. Initially each parent criticized the other – father was considered to be 'too hard' and mother to be 'too soft and indulgent'. It was clear enough that Colin's behaviour was a reaction to the parents' handling of him.

In the meetings aspects of the childhood experiences of both parents were explored, as these were influencing their views of parenthood. Father's childhood experiences included divorce of parents, mother's remarriage, a very strict stepfather and the disappearance of his natural father. He had not experienced a model of a fair, firm father and he 'wanted to do a better job' for his children. Mother had many brothers and sisters with unresolved issues of rivalry, sharing and alleged favouritism by her parents. She was determined that her children would not lose out and she indulged them, believing that saying 'no' to a child was a form of rejection.

Both father's firmness and mother's giving could be defined as aspects of a caring parent which needed to be modified and which for Colin's development (and that of his sister), needed to be balanced and united into a more consistent parental response. Other interventions were made in relation to the parents' perceptions of their own families of origin and these helped to strengthen their relationship and self-confidence. There were three meetings with the family, in which the child psychiatrist and the psychiatric social worker worked as co-therapists. The changes that the parents were able to make in their behaviour led to improvements in Colin's adjustment at school and reduced conflict at home.

Case example: Keith (aged 12)

School referred Keith because of his aggression towards other pupils and his erratic approach to school work; he was assessed as of good average intelligence. He lived with his parents and two elder school-age sisters. There had been concern about Keith's physical development in his pre-school years and this, combined with his being the only son and the youngest child, contributed to him being allowed special rules at home by his mother.

The whole family came to a school-based clinic and were seen by the psychiatric social worker, educational psychologist and year tutor. It became clear that there was marital conflict and that Keith had been drawn into it. Mother indulged and over-protected him, whilst father was peripheral, working long hours and resorting frequently to alcohol. Both sisters resented Keith's special dispensations and during the three meetings with the family, the sisters' shrewd observations were used to galvanize father into taking a more central role in the family and a closer interest in his son.

Changes in family roles were encouraged; father moved nearer to Keith and mother stepped back from her over-protective position. This represented a significant change in Keith's home environment, with father taking a lead and being validated in doing so.

A direct line of communication was established between school and father, so that firm containing limits were set. The meetings enabled family members to talk frankly with each other and a more consistent alliance was possible between the parents and their handling of Keith.

It is outside the scope of this chapter to describe the methods and techniques of clinical work with families and children. However the brief case examples are included in an attempt to give some flavour of the face-to-face situations occurring in the psychiatric social worker's work. Names of the children have been altered for reasons of confidentiality.

Chapter 8
The Role of the Speech Therapist

Julie Wagge

'*...the development of language is central to education*'.
(Plowden Report)

What is Speech Therapy?

Speech therapy is concerned with the development of communication and speech therapists are trained to manage all aspects of the
breakdown of communication skills in all age groups. The speech
therapist's training encompasses related areas of medicine, psychology, psycholinguistics, linguistics and education.

The majority of speech therapists are employed by District Health
Authorities. They are responsible for the assessment, diagnosis and
management of communication difficulties. Requests for speech
therapy are often through an open referral system. Referral can be
from a number of sources, the main ones being health visitors, parents, medical officers and teachers. The procedure generally followed is illustrated in Figure 8.1.

Speech therapists work in various settings – health centres, hospi-
tals, language units, special schools, special units, assessment units
and homes. Increasingly, the speech therapist is extending the role
of practitioners in the clinical setting and moving towards being
a member of the support team in schools.

A recent survey of speech therapy services (Cox, 1987) shows that
all health regions provide speech therapy input into all categories
of special schools. However not all categories are necessarily present
within each District Health Authority. Others however, have more
than one school or unit of any one category. Table 8.1 shows the
figures for speech therapy provision to special education.

Figure 8.1: Speech therapy procedure

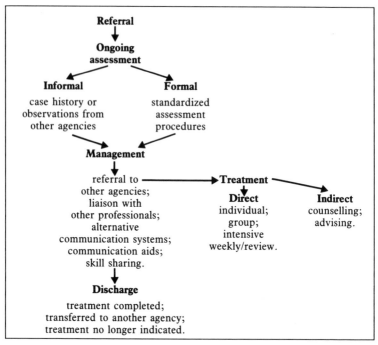

Table 8.1: Speech therapy provision to Special Education

Special education category	No. of schools/ units	No. of DHAs	Mean WTE provision per special school/unit	
			England/Wales	Scotland
Blind	10	10	.18	.05
Deaf	137	47	.12	.14
Physical handicap	103	71	.36	.30
Maladjusted	41	18	.11	.03
SLP	266	111	.30	.14
MLP*	420	112	.19	.17
Autistic	15	15	.48	–
Delicate	19	14	.17	–
Language disability	121	76	.65	.67
Other	155	53	.16	.38

*The category of Mild Learning Problems (MLP) includes 47 units in mainstream schools. 76 District Health Authorities may be seen to have reported the presence of educational units for children with language disabilities in their District, with a total number of 121 units. Thus 33 per cent of the sample had no provision for language disordered children within their authority, while 67 per cent were required to provide speech therapy for more than one unit.

Which Children need Speech Therapy?

Detailed assessment of speech and language levels is viewed within the context of the child's overall levels of development. Where a discrepancy in functioning is indicated then intervention is necessary. The speech therapist bases assessment on the normal framework of speech and language development. A diagnosis of the speech and language problem is then made.

Figure 8.2 shows the 'Language System'. A breakdown can occur at any one (or more than one) level.

Figure 8.2: The language system

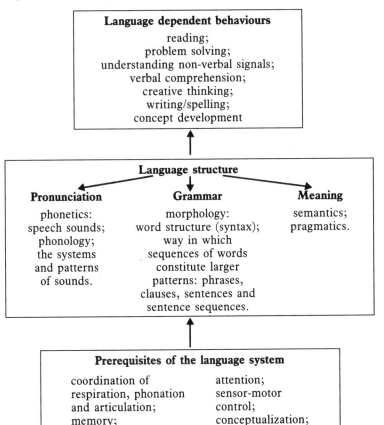

Assessments are not viewed in isolation, but within the context of the overall picture of the child's development and indeed within the normal pattern of the peer group, taking account of local variations in dialect, for example. A differential diagnosis is made between developmental *delay* (that is, where speech and language are developing along normal lines but at a slower rate than normal) and developmental *disorder* (where speech and language are not following the normal pattern of acquisition).

Receptive difficulties

One of the causes of receptive or verbal comprehensive difficulties, may of course be deafness. This may be of a permanent nature, or temporary and intermittent. A substantial number of children referred for speech therapy have experienced, or are experiencing, intermittent hearing loss as a result of middle ear infections.

It is not intended within the confines of a chapter to discuss the difficulties and remediation of hearing loss, as this is a huge topic in itself. The support of specialized teachers and speech therapists is an obvious necessity.

Receptive difficulties may occur in the absence of hearing loss. The terms 'dysphasia' or 'aphasia' are sometimes used where there is virtually no language development, or where the pattern of development is not normal. Such children generally demonstrate poor prerequisites for language development – poor auditory perception, poor auditory memory, slow processing of information, poor ability to cope with sequenced items. They often have poor rhythm. Symbolic development is poor, thus play may be limited early on. Such children are often very distractible and disorganized. Their attention span is generally limited.

All of these features tend to lead to poor concept development and difficulties with areas such as categorization and classification. They lead to obvious expressive problems.

Expressive difficulties

Difficulties with expressive speech and language fall into many categories. Figure 8.2 shows the breakdown of language structure into pronunciation, grammar and meaning.

a) *Pronunciation*

Phonetic difficulties, that is, problems with the production of speech sounds may result from one of two disabilities. In some cases, speech development is disordered as a result of neuromuscular abnormality. Thus oral movements are weak or uncoordinated. Articulation, phonation, resonance and prosody may be impaired. This problem is sometimes referred to as *dysarthria.*

In other cases, there may be an inability, or an impaired ability, to perform accurate or purposeful voluntary oral and/or articulatory movements, in the absence of any neurological damage. This problem is referred to as *dyspraxia.* There are often associated fine motor problems.

Some children have difficulties with the sequencing of sounds into meaningful units: these are referred to as phonological problems. Children follow a normal developmental process: for example 'cat' may be produced as 'ta' and then 'tat', and finally 'cat' during the normal progression. This process may be delayed or even disordered in some children where the rules governing the sounds and their combinations are missing.

b) *Grammar*

The breakdown in language development may occur at the level of grammar, and difficulties may be encountered with syntax and/or morphology. Again there is a normal pattern of development which may be delayed.

Very often, children's difficulties do not fit into clear-cut categories but affect different areas. For example, one child known to the author had severe phonological difficulties. At one stage in therapy, work concentrated on the /s/ sound and the child began to produce 'mouse', 'horse' and so on. However, the use of the final /s/ was not generalized to the morphological marker – 'cats' (plural), 'man's' (possessive), 'he's' (contraction of auxiliary), for example. Thus a morphological delay was also evident.

c) *Meaning*

Some children have particular problems acquiring vocabulary. Others have difficulty retrieving that vocabulary and display word-finding difficulties. These are characterized by 'groping' for words or talking around a subject but not naming it. Some of these children are helped by cueing processes.

Some children exhibit semantic and pragmatic difficulties. They may have difficulties with word meanings or with the relationships between words. Thus areas of 'oppositeness' and 'sameness' cause difficulties. They may have difficulty with sentence meaning and word order. They may have difficulty with utterance meaning. Problems occur with temporal and causal relationships. Difficulties are encountered with time vocabulary and sequencing and use of verb tenses. 'Why?' questions cause difficulties, as does the use of 'so' 'because' and 'if'.

The *structure* of the child's language may appear relatively normal but the *content* is not and difficulties are encountered with the use of language. Difficulties occur with reference, inference, categorization, specificity, and literal interpretation. The English language is fraught with phrases that are likely to cause problems with literal interpretation: for example, 'The man walked through the door'; 'The girl boiled the kettle'.

In addition to the areas mentioned, it should be noted that other difficulties requiring speech therapy include dysfluency, voice disorders, pitch disorders and difficulties with volume and resonance.

How Many Children need Speech Therapy?

Studies undertaken to identify the numbers of children with communication difficulties suggest that from five to ten per cent of school-age children need speech therapy. Webster and McConnell (1987), in their book *Children with Speech and Language Difficulties*, state that if 10 per cent of pre-school and school-age children have a language handicap which is serious enough to pose problems for themselves and their adult caretakers (as suggested by Crystal, 1982), then 'the implications for teachers working in ordinary schools is that approximately two or three children in every class can be expected to have a language difficulty of a greater or lesser degree'.

Dr. Geoffrey Ivimey, senior lecturer in the psychology and education of children with special needs at the Institute of Education is quoted in *Speech Therapy in Practice* (1986): 'Quite a large number of children have slight communication difficulties but these are not recognized at all. Sometimes the problems come out as difficulties with reading, writing or mathematics.' His research suggests that communication problems could affect up to 20 per cent of school children.

When to Refer for Speech Therapy

First and foremost it is important to say that if there is any concern about a child's speech and language development then a referral to a speech therapist should be made. The following list gives some pointers for referral. Children should be referred if:

- there are particular long-term or severe feeding problems;
- the child has only a few single words by two-years of age;
- speech is largely unintelligible by two and a half to three years;
- sentences are not appearing by two and a half years;
- there is an excessive amount of jargon (meaningless strings of speech) after 18 months;
- the amount of vocalizing decreases rather than steadily increases at any period of development;
- the child uses mostly vowel sounds in speech after 18 months of age;
- the child is embarrassed, disturbed or frustrated by his or her speech at any stage;
- the child is noticeably non-fluent at any age, particularly where there is parental concern;
- the voice is monotone, extremely loud, largely inaudible or of poor quality (hoarse or husky, for example);
- the pitch is not appropriate to the child's age and sex;
- there is noticeably hypernasality (too much nasal tone) or lack of nasal resonance;
- there is unusual word order or inappropriate grammar in connected speech ('it is going to a rains', for example);
- there is abnormal rhythm and inflection;
- there is inappropriate or unrealistic concern shown by parents or guardians; counselling may be necessary.

As stated previously, assessment of speech and language levels is viewed within the context of the child's overall levels of development. Referral should also be made bearing in mind the child's overall level of development. Clearly it is unrealistic to expect a child who is developmentally delayed to have reached age-appropriate

Table 8.2: Guidelines for the referral of pre-school children for speech and language assessment

Age	General and Social	Comprehension	Expression	Refer
18 months	Uses real and toy objects appropriately on self.	Points to familiar people and common objects on request. Understands simple commands (pick it up, fetch your shoes).	Uses at least 10 words meaningfully. Attempts imitation of new words and short phrases. Chatters nonsense to self, with wide range of different sounds.	If no comprehension of simple words (drink, biscuits). If not using a wide range of different sounds.
two years	Recognizes single-object pictures. Can match toy to picture. Acts out domestic activities (hoovering). Plays near other children.	Shows body parts on request. Associates two nouns in a simple command (put the *paper* in the *bin*).	Spontaneous words of approx. 50 words (understood by family). Joins two or more words (want drink, car gone).	If unable to follow simple commands. If not using approx. 20 words spontaneously.
two and a half years	Acts out sequences of everyday activities (meal – bath – bed). Watches others at play and may copy or join in briefly.	Understands simple short stories and conversation. Follows simple short story with pictures.	Combines three words. Begins to ask questions, use negatives and adjectives. Participates in rhymes and songs.	If not understanding two-noun commands (give the *doll* a *drink*). If not putting words together. If constantly echoing speech with little understanding.
three years	Understands activity in pictures.	Selects object pictures in relation to verb (Which one do we eat? Which one do we wear?). Understands common prepositions (in, on, under, behind).	Four- to five-word sentences which are intelligible to most people. Uses plurals and past tenses, not always correctly. Asks 'what', 'where', 'who' questions.	If not combining 3/4 words. If not understood by those in regular contact.

Table 8.2 cont.

Age	General and Social	Comprehension	Expression	Refer
four years	Some idea of past, present, future. Number concept of 2/3. Enjoys play with others. Imaginative role play with others (e.g. mothers and fathers, doctors and nurses).	Gives solutions to situations (what do you do when you're cold?). Identifies some colours comparatives and superlatives (big, bigger, biggest).	Uses complete sentences. Asks 'why', 'when' and sometimes 'how'. Relates stories and simple sequences of events. Most consonants used correctly. Some difficulty with long words and consonant combinations.	If speech difficult to understand. If omitting words or word endings (boys, boy*'s*, counts; coun*ting* coun*ted*). If unable to select 3 objects on request. If does not understand stories.
five years	Cooperates in group play.	Follows a simple story without pictures. Asks meaning of abstract words. Size, shape, colour, quantity and position words used as aids to reasoning and understanding.	Speech fully intelligible and all speech sounds present. Mastering irregular nouns and verbs (mice, men, drank, say). Can explain the meanings of simple words.	If unable to retain and follow command containing more than one instruction (put your painting on the radiator shelf and then hang your overall up). If unable to relate a short sequence of events. If having difficulty with any consonants or consonant combinations.

Note: Some hesitancy and sound repetition may occur for a brief period between two and a half to four years. If this is severe or prolonged, there should be referral for parental guidance.

Compiled by Miss M.J. Auckland, M.A., L.C.S.T. and Mrs J.A. Schmit B.Sc., M.Sc.

levels of speech and language development. However, this is not to say that developmentally delayed children do not need speech therapy.

Table 8.2 gives guidelines for referral of children up to five years of age.

The majority of five-year-olds entering mainstream schools have reached a level of linguistic competence whereby they are able to express themselves fluently, grammatically and with only minor immaturities of speech. Where this is not the case, referral may be indicated.

Difficulties producing consonants or consonant combinations are generally easy to pick up, but it can be more difficult to recognize the child who is experiencing comprehension problems. Such a child can often present as either disobedient (attention level is poor and the child often fails to carry out commands) or reserved and quiet – (he or she makes few demands and carries out tasks by following the lead of other children). Thus it can take some time to identify the root cause of a child's behaviour as possibly being a language problem. This, therefore, highlights the importance of incorporating the screening of language development into other screening in the classroom.

Children who are experiencing difficulties with the meaning of language, as discussed earlier, may not be identified until they are in school. Thus teachers should be aware of the areas mentioned such as 'oppositeness' and categorization. The lack of an appropriate sense of humour in verbal situations may be indicative of difficulties with meaning.

How to Refer

The majority of District Speech Therapy services have an open referral system, the teacher can refer directly to the speech therapist, having obtained parental consent to do so. If the name and base of work of the local speech therapist is unknown, then referral should be made to the service coordinator, usually called the District Speech Therapist. The School Health Department should be able to give the necessary details of base for the District Speech Therapist. Many areas have referral forms for use by teachers. An example is shown in Figure 8.3.

Figure 8.3: Example of a teacher's referral form

Child's name .... Date of birth ....
Address .... Telephone number ....
GP ....
School ....
Reason for referral (brief description of problem) ....
....
....
Further information
Source of referral .... Date of referral ....

Where available, any known history is helpful, as well as information about hearing tests. It may be a good idea to consult the school nurse about referral, as she is able to make the referral, give medical information and liaise easily with the local speech therapist. The signature of a parent or guardian giving consent for the referral is often requested. This is to ensure that the teacher has met with the parents or guardians and discussed with them their anxieties about the child's language development, prior to making a referral.

Provision for Children with Speech and Language Difficulties

Figure 8.4 shows a continuum of provision for children with speech and language difficulties as given by Webster and McConnell (1987).

The speech therapist in a supporting role

As stated, the speech therapist is increasingly a member of the support team in schools. As with all the members, this role within the team may be variable. The therapist work in the classroom supporting children with speech and language difficulties; the child may be withdrawn for individual or group activities; work may be

Figure 8.4: A continuum of provision for children with speech and language difficulties

Placement in a mainstream class – occasional monitoring and help from language specialist or speech therapist.

↓

Mainstream class with additional help in some subject areas from language support teacher, remedial specialist plus speech therapy.

↓

Ordinary class with tutorial help: Child is withdrawn for extra help by a specialist teacher or teacher's assistant on a daily or weekly basis across a range of subjects, with speech therapy.

↓

Resource unit in a mainstream school: special class with varying degrees of integration in ordinary groups. Usually combined with more intensive language activities with speech therapy.

↓

Special school as a base with part-time integration into ordinary classes and speech therapy input.

↓

Full-time special school with intensive specialist teaching and speech therapy.

From Webster and McConnell, 1987.

done in conjunction with a teaching assistant implementing language programmes; or there may be less direct child-contact following assessment and more full involvement in the planning of approaches through discussion.

Where a child's special educational needs are primarily speech and language difficulties; or where there is a more general profile of learning difficulties with particular reference to specific speech and language, the speech therapist may act as a catalyst for the support team.

Corinne Hayes (1986) states that 'The first task of all team members is to communicate with each other and to create a common understanding of the area in which they will be pooling their expertise.' Communication between the team members is essential to the success of any supportive programme. Effective means of exchange of information and availability of time for such exchanges are necessary for this success.

Who are the members of the team?

The team members will of course vary from situation to situation but are likely to include teachers, specialist adviser or support teacher, educational psychologist, speech therapist, teaching assistants, nursery staff, and parents. The vital role of parents in language *acquisition* is well documented; their input where language *difficulties* occur is also important. A large proportion of the child's communication takes place in the home situation and therefore intervention in isolation from the home environment is likely to be less effective. In many situations, the speech therapist provides a link between home and school. Having a child experiencing communication difficulties in the family may require the speech therapist to play a counselling role.

Corinne Hayes (1986) states that 'It is essential that, in dealing with a common problem, each member of the team should clearly understand the aims and skills of the other members.' In addition to the understanding of aims and skills, understanding of the child's developmental stage is important. In the case of speech and language difficulties, it is likely that the speech therapist will take responsibility for advising the other team members about the nature and effects of these areas of difficulty.

Assessment

The assessment of the child's abilities is also a team function. It is important that a holistic approach is taken and that the child's speech and language levels are viewed within the context of the child's general development.

In order to have as full an understanding as possible of the child, it is important for the therapist to have knowledge of his or her day-to-day linguistic needs and functioning. Thus, those people involved in the child's daily routines at home and in school are in the best place to provide examples for assessment. In the experience of the author, the transcription of spontaneous language by someone in daily contact with the child (such as the welfare assistant) is far more meaningful for the monitoring of generalization of learned linguistic skills than is the use of standardized assessments.

Record keeping

Ongoing records are vital to monitor progress and as a means of identifying successful methods of intervention. Methods of record keeping vary in establishments depending on the individuals involved, and their training. Tape recordings and transcriptions are useful, as are daily 'diaries' of activities and performances. An index system of activities for various areas of remediation acts as a useful catalogue for ongoing programmes. Where commercially available kits (such as the *Derbyshire Language Scheme*; Knowles and Masidlover, 1982) are useful, records sheets may need to be supplemented and tailored to the individual child. Profiles of the child's needs, abilities and provision are useful where various professionals are involved. The important factor is that the means of recording is understood by and relevant to all those involved. Thus the speech therapist may need to share linguistic skills.

Figure 8.5 shows an example of a 'Profile of linguistic needs' drawn up by the author and used in a middle-school language unit. The profile was used to give an overview of areas needing the attention of the language teachers. Thus some linguistic knowledge was assumed. The profile is an amalgamation of parts of other profiles such as 'Language assessment, remediation and screening procedure' (LARSP) and PRISM-L, (Crystal, 1982).

Programmes

Programmes for speech and language intervention fall mainly into two categories – commercially available kits and individually tailored programmes. In the author's experience in most cases, a combination of the two is often most successful.

Figure 8.5: Profile of linguistic needs

Family name: .... First name/s: .... Date of birth: ....

PHONOLOGY

Plosives	Approximants	/c/
Affricates	Vowels	/c/
Fricatives	Diphthongs	/c/
Nasals		

Clusters
Process analysis

MORPHOLOGY

-ing	3s	N irreg. reg.
plural	gen	V irreg. reg.
-ed	n't	
-en	'cop	

SYNTAX

Clause

		Phrase	
SVO	Coord	Det N	Cop
SVA	Passive	Pro N	Aux
QXY	VS(X+)	Adj N	Neg
tag	Complement	Prep N	
	Conn.		

PRAGMATICS

Interactional turn-taking
exchanges initiating
responding
continuing
attention-getting devices

Transactional relevance
informativeness
accuracy/truthfulness

Skills describing
narrating
inferencing
establishing reference
ability to repair
conversational breakdown

SEMANTICS

Vocabulary – recall/new
Temporal sequencing
Cause and effect perception

Minor Lexemes
Social (e.g. oh, thank you) Relational (e.g. I, am)
Avoidance (e.g. whatsit)

Major Lexemes

Man			Body	Health
Clothing			Food	
Moving		Making/Doing	Happening	Living
Having			Thinking	Feeling
Sound		Smell	Taste	Touch
Language			Imagination	
Recreation	Sight		Music	Art
Road	Occasions	Shows	Water	Fuel
Animals	Rail	Air		Insects
Flowers		Birds	Fish	Light
Colour		Trees		Water
Building		Fire		Containers
Quantity	Furniture	Tools		Shape
Time	Measurement	Size		State
Government		Location		
Space	Law	Education	Religion	Business manufacture
Other	World	Minerals		Weapons	Money

VOICE/PROSODIC FEATURES

Intonation	Speed of speech
Voice quality	Pause
Loudness	Rhythm

ANY OTHER COMMENTS

Non-verbal eye contact
self confidence

J. Wagge

The supporting role of the speech therapist, where programmes are being used, is to suggest activities and to help evaluate progress. This is why record keeping is essential. Master copies of activity sheets, games and so on, should always be kept in order to build up base resources. Whilst programmes are not necessarily transferable, activities may be used in different ways with different children. A good understanding of the aims and objectives of tasks is needed by the person carrying them out in order for them to be successful: it is the speech therapist's responsibility to ensure that this is the case. This emphasizes the role of the speech therapist as skill sharer: an understanding of the areas of difficulty and an understanding of the aims of remediation leads to a more successful programme.

An important aspect of programmes is that wherever possible, their content should be meaningful. Thus activities integrated into the curriculum can be particularly successful. Where the language being used is curriculum-based there is likely to be far more transfer into spontaneous conversation. The model of the integrated day lends itself to this approach particularly well. Topic work can be adapted to work on specific linguistic skills. To this end, a topic such as 'myself' might provide excellent opportunities for comprehension work, sequencing activities, vocabulary and semantic work, and auditory memory tasks. Familiar activities such as cloze procedure can be incorporated.

The way in which programmes are carried out is obviously variable. Activities may be carried out in groups or individually. The composition of groups may vary, and the person facilitating the group needs to be aware of each child's strengths and weaknesses in order to gear tasks at the right level. It may sometimes be beneficial to include in the group children with no language problems. These children provide good models for the others and this also helps to make the language activities an integrated part of the curriculum.

Another important consideration is the availability of suitable accommodation in which to work. In view of the poor attention and distractability of some of the children, a quiet space may be needed. The timing of the support of the speech therapist is another factor which is likely to be variable. In some cases it needs to be ongoing and regular, in other cases it may be intensive to begin with and then gradually lessen to regular but less frequent monitoring sessions.

The intervention of a speech therapist in the classroom setting can have very significant additional benefits in terms of increased mutual understanding and appreciation of the work of the professionals involved. Such intervention can also provide a useful form of in-service training.

Looking to the Future

The implementation of the 1981 Education Act and the subsequent integration of children with special needs into mainstream schools has undoubtedly put an extra strain on already stretched support services such as the speech therapy service. The evaluation and careful monitoring of projects is essential in order to quantify and qualify the need for further resources and staffing where necessary.

There can be little doubt that a successful team approach achieves far more than individuals working in isolation. It is therefore essential that better training for all professionals is undertaken to promote understanding of each others' areas of expertise, leading to the development of an integrated team.

Chapter 9
Broadening the Role of
Support Teaching

John Dwyfor Davies and Pat Davies

The proliferation of support schemes designed to maximize the learning experiences of children with special needs in ordinary schools has sharpened awareness of the qualitative experiences necessary for successful integration. No longer is it adequate to abdicate responsibility to a 'specialist' teacher. Nor is it acceptable for the class teacher to assume total responsibility in the name of 'normalization' or 'integration'.

Teacher energy in supporting these schemes is often dissipated by the vast array of other professional pressures confronting them. Consequently, the frustration resulting from practical constraints and thwarted benevolence can only be resolved through a radical and innovative reappraisal of existing resources. Within this, support agencies will need to meet the expectations of individual teachers, whilst drawing on the skills and knowledge that they already possess.

Currently, support teachers are having to review their own practice in the light of both teacher expectation and emerging research, which suggests that traditional remedial methods are of limited value in the long term. For example, Tobin and Pumfrey (1976) conclude that although progress in reading is possible by working with reluctant readers in withdrawal groups, it is seldom maintained without continuing support. Whereas the encouragement of parental support schemes, along with a review of peer group support, can lead to increased and sustained motivation and progress in children's learning. Jenny Hewison (1987), in a follow-up study of the original Haringey Reading project, found that those children who received extra parental help were reading well, three years after the project had finished. This highlights the pivot on which effective development rests. The main task within this reappraisal is that of identifying existing positive, supportive practice and to progress from this point.

A major dilemma is that of marrying the dual roles of support and change agent. The reappraisal of how all children learn well demand that a school reviews its current practice and provision. The central task is that of identifying first principles in such a way that it can incorporate the support and imagination of the entire school staff.

There are contrasting views as to how whole school practice can best be developed. On the one extreme, a 'top-down' approach may be advocated, whereby the initiative is taken by the head and senior staff. This is then imposed on the staff and an explicit directive given as to how the identified goals are to be achieved. If the head teacher clearly promotes a policy of equal opportunity and respect for each child, this must have a powerful effect on the attitudinal bias of the whole staff. On the other hand, the initiative may come from a few teachers who enthuse and inspire others to question the efficacy of their current practice – a 'bottom-up' approach. Some teachers, through personal commitment and drive for achievement, attract and encourage others with a similar ideology and interests to pursue a reflective stance and question many assumptions on which practice is based.

A fusion of both these approaches is more likely to succeed. To initiate this process of reappraisal of existing policy and practice, it may be necessary to develop an environment in which all concerned can feel secure enough to explore issues with mutual professional respect. Within such a climate, priorities can be identified leading to organizational changes which can be creative, constructive and enriching to staff and children alike. Such a climate can only be arrived at when the head teacher is committed to such a philosophy. Without such professionalism, the prognosis for change is poor. Developing a whole-school policy involves much more than focusing on individual curricular areas. More fundamentally, the school will need to consider the total philosophy upon which it bases its practice. It is within this coordinated framework that the rest will function.

Underpinning all this are the attitudes held by the staff. These too will need to be made explicit and explored openly in an atmosphere of mutual support. Mia Kellmer Pringle (1976) noted teacher warmth and enthusiasm as attributes closely associated with pupil achievement. Similarly, progress on refining policies regarding specific curricular issues can only be achieved when a climate of warmth, respect, value and humour permeates staff perceptions of their responsibilities and their role.

The Role of the Special Needs Advisory and Support Teacher in Helping Effect Change

In addition to the direct support offered to children requiring individual teaching, the following roles are vital to broaden perceptions and dialogue in our schools.

To maximize opportunities

Effective support teaching is based on the ability to relate well to different people with their varied expertise and expectations. If support teachers can communicate openly, free from jargon and mystique, with respect for the views of professionals, parents and children, they are more likely to succeed in widening discussion both at formal meetings and informally in staffrooms.

To act as a catalyst in staff debate

Whilst the support teacher is not a permanent member of any one school team, acceptance as an equal in several schools can enable him or her to offer a broad perspective and act as a catalyst by initiating or stimulating change. If class teachers have worked closely with the support teacher and developed a feeling of team-work and shared responsibility, the result is often a strengthening of resolve and collaboration. A willingness to review each other's contribution to the child's learning comes from a regular exchange of observation and information, and joint planning.

To promote an awareness and respect for individual differences

As well as exploring issues arising from the inability of some children to respond to the curriculum on offer, a major element of the role is that of identifying implications which emanate from both the *overt* and the *hidden* curriculum operating within the school. Galloway and Goodwin (1987) observed that support teachers can spend a large amount of time working with individuals or small groups who are a cause for concern. They acknowledge that individual pupils may need attention and help in their own right, but this cannot be divorced from attention to wider issues of school policy and practice. The support teacher must help create an ethos of responsibility and respect and must actively 'help promote awareness and respect for individual differences'. Whole-school policy can only develop through dialogue that allows all members of staff to reflect upon their personal and corporate constructs: these will have been acquired through day-to-day practice and circumstances. Support teachers need to enable school staffs to engage in the process of redefining educational success and to value children as individuals.

To facilitate developments in classroom practice and in-service education

Discussions centred on curriculum areas such as approaches to reading, the writing process, language enrichment, etc., often begin informally in classrooms and may later be formalized and lead to a broader exchange of school-focused in-service considerations, involving a wider staff participation and interprofessional exchange. Teachers are far more likely to consider new approaches when they have worked successfully with the support teacher and have an incentive to evaluate positive patterns.

This may be continued at the Resource Centre and can take many forms, such as talks or discussions led by invited speakers; workshops led by local teachers to encourage an exchange of good practice already existing in many schools. The ultimate aim is to establish networks of interested colleagues so that the support team will gear their input to the needs of each group and will take responsibility for sustaining momentum.

From Theory to Practice

Supporting school-based developments

Many schools have already invited support teachers to help develop initiatives. These have been wide in nature and have allowed the role to be perceived in a broad light. In many small village schools in East Oxfordshire, parental involvement has been fostered and is now an integral feature of the schools' policies. Each head teacher targeted the parents of pre-school and infant children and considered ways in which they could strengthen existing tenuous links between pre-school agencies and themselves. This was achieved by staff discussing their aims and identifying ways in which they could validate the role of parents as educators. What eventually emerged was the growth of a whole tier of support. Meetings were carefully planned to enable a rich exchange of views and queries to surface. They took place in the evening in the local playgroup, with pre-school workers discussing what they had on offer. Parents and infant teachers visited the playgroup children during morning sessions, whilst the support teacher took the infant class. The support teacher also took the class to enable the head and class teacher to exchange information with new parents. In this way, the special needs teacher was seen from the beginning by new parents as a support and not an extractor of 'remedials'. Also, when specific projects were planned on writing, maths or reading, parents felt secure when they saw an agreed and consistent approach from all the professionals concerned with their child's learning.

Within a large primary school in an Educational Priority Area of Oxfordshire, the initial response by the support teacher was to requests, from a number of class teachers, to work with groups of children who were struggling to acquire literacy skills. An evaluation of classroom practice was initiated by the newly-appointed head teacher and literacy was identified as an area of concern throughout the school. The head teacher believed that the large numbers of children needing a vast input by both internal and external support staff could best be helped through effecting a whole-school approach to reading and language, which encouraged teacher/parental participation and support for their children's reading development. Parallel to this was a review of the reading opportunities on offer to each class group, with reference to a close analysis of the scope of literature and materials available and of teacher expectation.

The support teacher was invited to initiate three separate projects over a year-long period with a reception class, a first year junior class and a third year junior class. During this time the support teacher worked with children and class teachers in identifying ways of encouraging motivation and enjoyment of story and literature and on assessing the role of adults (including teachers, classroom-helpers and parents) in this process.

To effect this systematic and potentially threatening review, it was necessary to solicit the views – and the support – of the entire school staff. A series of staff meetings based on the principles outlined above, explored not only the beliefs and rationale underlying the practice of individual staff members, but also current thinking and recent research findings on factors influencing children's learning, such as the Partnership between Parents, Children and Teachers (PACT), Liz Waterland's 'apprenticeship' approach to reading (Waterland, 1985), and so on.

The support teacher was involved throughout this exercise, which was designed to enable teachers to sharpen their thinking and to crystallize positive directions for development. Many staff members were beginning to voice their concern about difficulties in articulating a rationale on which their practice was based. This openness was only possible because of the supportive ethos that had developed within the school.

A series of subsequent meetings were used to explore related issues, including learning theories and comparative classroom practices, resources, record-keeping, the role of other adults in the classroom, peer group support, ways of communicating with parents.

The head and support teachers (both internal and external) collated the ideas which had emerged to date, and used them to draw up the documents which are shown overleaf.

Figure 9.1: Working document – Aims

Aims

To explore the value of encouraging teacher/parental commitment to their childrens approach to reading. During the Autumn term could you invite the parents of each child in your class, to discuss with them ways of encouraging home reading – to, with, or by their child.

   Choose whichever of these suggestions suits you best; *or,* develop your own ideas:

* Informal invitations to groups of parents to come into class for a cup of tea and cakes (perhaps involving the children in the baking), to set a date for another meeting, without their children, to talk about ways they can help their child enjoy and read stories. Some parents will not turn up, so they may need to be contacted individually.
* When you hold an individual parents' evening in the Autumn term, try and make a point of discussing approaches to reading, inviting questions and agreeing a plan of action.
* Make an individual approach to parents; when and where to be mutually agreed.
* Think of ways to record what happens: which parents respond, which have to be pursued.
* Aim to review staff experiences at the end of term.

Figure 9.2: Working document – Practical help

Practical help

* Review existing central stock and distribution of the best of the books to each infant class.
* Head teacher to order more Kaleidoscope collections, Story Chest or picture/story books identified by teachers as desirable.
* Infant staff to spend some time at the Resource Centre, reviewing the range of early picture and story books.
* Plastic wallets to be ordered or book-bags made, if preferred.
* Please think about the wording of phrases to slip into a home reading folder; for example, 'Your child may need you to read this story to him/her', 'Your child would like to read this story to you, but may need some help.' These will be produced ready for distribution.
* Design a selection of reading leaflets to use as a guide for parents. Examples from other schools can be found in folder in the staffroom.
* Record/card/sheet to be designed and included in the reading folder. Bring any examples that you find work well for you, to the next staff meeting.
* Ongoing discussion at this term's staff meetings on the need for a structured or core group of books in each classroom, which could provide a backbone for children's reading progress, as a sort of safety net?

Figure 9.3: Working document – Parental involvement

Other possible ways of involving parents in the reading process

- Discuss value of incentives: for example, child colours a section of a picture each time a book is shared. Ask parent to pop in when the picture is taking shape, to see how it is going. Or are the story books a reward in themselves?
- Encourage parents to come into the classroom, to join the class story group and listen to the story read by the teacher; when confident, suggest parent read to two or three children and talk about the value of small-group story-telling.
- Develop and make activities for parents to use with their children at home. (The Resource Centre would make up any ideas.)
- Give children who have started to read choices about the help they receive; for example, 'Do you like reading to an adult best? Or to your friend?'; 'Do you enjoy reading to someone from the same book?'; 'Do you like reading to younger children?'
- Pair children for reading – either in the same class, or juniors reading stories to infants.
- Story swop: offer several story titles to be read by class teachers and encourage children to choose which group they go to.
- Use of local library: take small groups of children and parents along for, for example, the last half-hour of one day per fortnight.
- Invite parents to come into class at the end of one afternoon per week, to read to their child and select a story to take home.
- Stop calling books 'reading books'.
  Just call them **books**!

Ultimately, the project developed a form which enabled the staff to refine and establish more appropriate strategies and procedures, both within the classroom and for sharing books at home. This was not an easy or uniformly-accepted process. On the contrary, this questioning of established routine was disturbing to some members of staff. The very act of *asking* individual class reachers to make explicit long-held views caused ripples of uncertainty. However, every opportunity was taken by the head and support teachers to allow comment, query and doubt to surface, and at the end of the term a review was undertaken. (See Figure 9.4.)

There was a very positive response to the questionnaire and every respondent agreed that it was important to identify what had created the lively and open interchange at each parents meeting. This was encouraging as some class teachers had felt insecure about present-

Figure 9.4: Project review

> **Review of initial stages of shared reading project through teacher questionnaire**
>
> **Aims:** To explore as a staff, through a series of staff meetings and informal discussion, ways in which young children learn to read and how we can develop skills to enable parents to contribute to this process.
>   What have been your experiences in the following area:
>
> - How did you approach parents and and did you organize subsequent meetings?
> - What system of sharing books have you settled on?
> - What successes/benefits have you experienced? Is there any evidence that children in your class are more switched on to books?
> - What difficulties have you experienced?
> - Do you feel that the 'system' is working? If not, what support do you feel you need next term?
> - How do you plan to sustain parental interest?
> - Do the children continue to want to take books home?

ing these ideas to groups of parents and had asked the support teacher to lead in. Care had been taken to make each parent feel welcome and valued and in the more successful meetings, parents had felt confident enough to express not only their queries, but also to voice their criticisms without fear of reproach or of being patronized.

Most parents expressed distinct stages in their understanding of the rationale behind the meetings. Some expressed difficulty in understanding the reasons why teachers were questioning such basic processes, as how children learn to read. Others were uneasy at the role that they were being asked to undertake. Then there emerged interest and surprise in the simplicity of the suggestions made. The acknowledgement that their ongoing interest and encouragement would positively help their child's learning was deeply rewarding. This was reinforced by the fact that this message was being conveyed by teachers. Many parents expressed interest and delight at the range and quality of books now available to their children.

All the teachers, with one exception, felt that there was great enthusiasm for the new approach. They noted that parents were eager to dip into the books – they were as enthusiastic about the stories and rhymes as were the children. Also, children were actively reading to brothers, sisters and grandparents, as well as to parents. The discussion back in class inspired continued interest and one class teacher felt that there had already been an improvement in actual performance – as well as a greater interest in books: 'Children look forward to story time and cannot wait to read their stories to me (and to the other children) as they come into school each morning.'

Some worries still persisted, especially regarding the need for more resources, in contacting some parents and in maintaining a routine, but the overall conclusion was that the special combination of extra motivation and practice had been very powerful.

Confirmation through Practice

What was encouraging was the discovery that, by questioning long-established approaches to children's learning, teachers were seeing the same results as they had read about in numerous shared reading projects (in Haringey, Salford and Leicester, for example). Paul Widlake (1986) describes the beneficial consequences of these approaches:

It is probable that good results achieved through these approaches can be adequately explained by the psychoanalysts Bettelheim and Zelan (1982), during an account of their own non-interventionist procedures for helping emotionally-disturbed children overcome reading difficulties. They suggest that a positive attitude promotes reading, because it is based on a reciprocal agreement that enhances a child's self respect around reading. Shared reading programmes all emphasized the parents' role in ignoring the child's errors, but immediately offered a further correct model. In accepting children's misreadings, enthusiasts for this approach may have stumbled upon an important learning principle.

The next stift in awareness was to establish that reading in class must *continue* to hold a high priority and that the material and purpose must be meaningful for *each* pupil. Also that sending books home and communicating readily with parents would require a high level of organization on the part of the teacher.

Divergent Views: A Professional Right to Question Current Assumptions

As the staff monitored the response of the children, debate centred around those children with learning and adjustment difficulties. To what extent had the new approaches enthused the large numbers of children who had been struggling to learn to read? Did the greater range of intrinsically interesting literature, now offered as a legitimate alternative, improve motivation and learning? Did these 'real' books 'offer much more, to which a child could respond at an affective level', as Bruner (1974) suggests? Once again, the staff had to be prepared to observe the children's response very carefully and indeed some teachers could not let go of some hierarchical 'remedial' schemes, with their accompanying repertoire of flashcards, work-sheets and repetitous utterances.

However, these teachers were prepared to compromise and began to offer a wider range of literature to their pupils; they continued to discuss alternative ways of improving attitudes to reading and learning. By feeling confident amongst their colleagues, they were able to express their reservations about what they saw as a lack of structure in the newer approach. Indeed their arguments served to remind the more passionate advocates of meaningful literature, of the need to review methods for teaching phonic skills and other strategies necessary for purposeful reading.

Open review of existing practice: the support teacher's role

Many small village schools in East Oxfordshire, and numerous schools throughout the country, are at a parallel stage in examining the implications of their analysis of what constitutes an effective reading/language policy – not only for partnership between parents and teachers, but also for motivation and self-image. If all children made good progress, teachers would have little incentive to review their existing curriculum and teaching methods. Some class teachers enquired about the value and methodology of peer group reading, as they felt it was more natural for a child to read with a friend or a class-mate than with an adult. The support teacher was able to dispel anxieties that the more efficient readers would be 'wasting time' by supporting their less fluent peers.

This was done by offering articles written by practising teachers, or by arranging exchange visits to classrooms where group reading had become an integral part of the curriculum. These teachers observed that there had been an improvement in performance – in accuracy, interest and confidence – in both 'tutee' and 'tutor'. Shared reading provided the better reader with an opportunity to practice and refine his own reading skills, whilst at the same time fostering a sense of worth and responsibility – as well as fun in working together. As more teachers tried out their own version of peer-supported reading, they noticed a change in atmosphere in the classroom: children voluntarily shared stories, plays and rhymes with each other. Visitors and parents commented on the lively interchange now occurring in classrooms. At subsequent meetings, parents told how this practice was continuing at home: their intuitive reaction was that reading to a friend (or brother or sister) had enhanced confidence and enjoyment as well as competence in their children. This again illustrates the importance of motivation as a major determinant in learning. When an atmosphere of praise, recognition and value permeates a classroom, all children benefit socially as well as academically.

Developing a Congruent Approach

Galloway and Goodwin (1987) suggest that children with learning and adjustment difficulties expose the shortcomings of their school's organization, structure, curriculum and interpersonal relationships. But if schools can begin to deal with the underlying *cause* of these tensions, then it is likely to benefit all pupils and relationships with parents.

If support teachers are able to encourage emerging trends by recognizing that learning from each other – adults as well as children – is not 'cheating', then a whole range of possibilities will open up. Although the above examples of reviewing whole-school policy are confined to literacy, they have major implications for the curriculum offered to all pupils: should the uniqueness of each child require that he or she be taught separately, or can cooperative learning be more powerful? By working cooperatively, children learn to discuss possibilities, to listen to other points of view, to explain, to persuade, to take turns, to resolve disagreements and that each has a contribution to make. If parents and pupils see external and internal staff working as a team, confidence in their message is also more likely.

Support teachers soon learn through experience to identify those head teachers and class teachers within schools who are supportive of change and those who actively wish to share challenges. As visitors, support teachers must be sensitive to the needs of both individual teachers and groups and must also be sharply aware of underlying messages and hidden reservations. Full frontal attacks on teachers who are uncertain and defensive deplete and absorb energy and can harden resistance to proposed change. Change requires additional energy, sensitivity and talent and so the support teacher must nurture those individuals who wish to review aspects of their practice. When a headteacher endorses such teamwork and has personal and organizational skills to create a coherent view, then drive and morale are powerfully boosted.

Reflection, review and restructuring can only occur when class teachers, who are the most valuable resource that a school has, further develop skills in cooperating and liaising. It is the role of the support teacher to validate each attempt at cooperation and to encourage strong personal support relationships among team members. Cohesion will not grow until *all* teachers are seen to have prime responsibility for finding ways of supporting children with learning and adjustment difficulties. Establishing a whole-school policy that gives priority to the child as an individual learner is an enormous task, which is fraught with obstacles and frustration. Respect and concern for the rights and welfare of individual pupils is a long-term responsibility that requires consistent monitoring and refining. When teams of professionals believe confidently that their schools are not merely institutions concerned with the narrow curriculum of the 'three Rs', striving to achieve prescribed benchmarks, but rather that they are places in which positive social attitudes are formed and individuals valued – *then* the sharing of responsibility will enrich everyone involved in a very powerful way.

Chapter 10
Parental Perspectives on Support

Sarah Sandow

Extensive research has shown that children benefit from the interest and involvement of parents in their education (McConkey, 1985). Professionals are increasingly embracing the notion of partnership and joint responsibility in day-to-day encounters with parents in an attempt to harness the knowledge, skills and understanding that they have of their own children. An even greater sense of professionalism and sensitivity is needed to understand the complex interplay of roles and responsibilities when negotiating with the parents of children with special needs. This chapter examines the perceptions of parents and professionals and draws on the authors' recent research in looking at factors which enhance or inhibit the establishment of genuine partnership.

For the past 30 years – if not longer – professionals have been seeking to assist parents in the care of children with learning and behaviour difficulties. In doing so, they have defined the problems in their own terms. Where parents have joined the discussion (Hannam, 1975; Brock, 1976) they have usually been professionals in their own right, and able to convey to other professionals a view of their situation which is seen by those professionals as articulate and eloquent enough to command respect. Thomas (1982) described a situation in which the territory of each profession is mapped out with techniques, technical language and value systems that weave a web of mystique around the concept of 'handicap' and at the same time reinforce it. The use of jargon or 'specialist' language, the professional monopoly of decision-making and the traditional unequal relationship between parents and providers enable the members of different professions to communicate with one another. However, these factors exclude parents from what is seen as a 'professional problem'.

The views of people who have been through the professional process are sometimes treated as useful, supplementary anecdotal material or rejected as being too subjective and personalised, lacking research rigour or simply dismissed as the outpouring of an atypical or highly disaffected individual (Thomas, 1982, p.19)

Defining the Role of Parents

The definition of the parent's role has changed over time, according to the professional group which has had the most powerful influence over the lives of the parents and their children. In the case of children with severe or moderate learning difficulties, or with physical or sensory handicaps, it has reflected the shift in responsibility for assessment from *medical* to *psychological* personnel. Where children with behavioural or emotional problems are concerned, the parents' role has reflected the preoccupations of medicine, psychiatry, social work and education.

However, all of these relationships have been based on the idea that the difficulty being experienced by the parents and the children has its origin in one of the following areas:

- within the child himself;
- within the relationship established between the parent and the child;
- within the parent's inability to cope with the established (that is, 'professional') view of the problem.

Parents are commonly described as 'coming to terms with', 'accepting' or 'not accepting' a situation, or indeed a child; refusal to do so may be regarded as a pathological reaction. At the opposite extreme, parents who do *not* react powerfully to the situation have been largely ignored, many professionals refusing to believe that such a serious problem can be other than devastating in their eyes. Gath (1972) recognized this, when she wrote of families where the handicapped child presented less severe problems than the conditions of social or financial deprivation which existed for their parents. Humphreys (1987) discusses the 'silent majority' which is largely satisfied with the services offered and does not seek to participate actively in the educational process.

Some parents' views of professionals are coloured by the difficult relationships formed between them at the time when a child's problems are first discovered: Glendinning (1983) gives many examples of this. Doctors in particular are cited as being reluctant to admit the existence of a problem; eventually, when the problem *is* at last admitted, the emphasis may be on the 'something wrong' with the *child* rather than on the adaptations necessary within the *services* offered. Booth (1981) argues that this is the first stage in the marginalization of children with learning difficulties. The professionals are at first dismissive and reluctant to identify a difficulty; later, they place the onus '...on the parents to adjust the phasing of the expectations they hold of the child'. Thus the parents are gradually led to 'accept' the exceptional nature of their child, and to see themselves as the parents of an essentially different individual.

Having acquired this status, parents of children with learning or behavioural difficulties become increasingly different from the 'normal population' – not least in the number and nature of their encounters with professionals. These encounters reinforce the parents in their developing view of the deviance of their child, whether this is described as the consequence of a specific syndrome or as a result of some distorted family relationship. Some may come to depend on this difference from other, apparently 'normal', families and professionals have sought ways of making the process a positive rather than a negative one. Thus it has become fashionable to describe the relationship between these parents and the professionals as a 'partnership'. According to the conventional wisdom the partnership is an equal one: however, the disparity in weight of responsibility and the 'uneven balance of power' (Thomas, 1982) between parents and professionals makes this equality seem improbable.

Parents of children with severe learning difficulties, who have been in the forefront of the growing campaign for more involvement in their childrens' education, have a very special and intense experience of professional help which alters, for better or worse, all their future encounters. Parents whose children have less obvious learning difficulties may respond differently. Although greater in number, they have traditionally been less involved with education and, as Tomlinson remarks, the connection between low socioeconomic status, mild educational subnormality and badly behaved children has probably contributed to inadequate parental involvement and consultation. (Tomlinson, 1981).

Parents whose children have moderate learning difficulties may have had little to do with educational personnel apart from their child's teacher, and even this contact is infrequent. Parents often expect such contacts to be occasions where teachers complain about the child, or where they are 'sent for and told' by the teacher about his or her problems (Tomlinson, 1981).

Parents: customers or suppliers?

In the context of the ordinary school, parents can be described either as 'customers' or as 'suppliers': there is often a social class difference between these two. 'The ruling class and its schools are articulated mainly through a market, while the working class and its schools are articulated mainly through a bureaucracy, (Connell *et al.*, 1982). Customers share with the providers a common consensus about the service on offer, which provides a means of creating an end-product according to the needs of 'society'. They see themselves as representing that 'society' and (either because they are the fee payers or because they see the relationship between taxation and education) they feel the existence of 'rights'. The suppliers, on the other hand, perceive the relationship quite differently. They provide material (their children) for teachers to work on. The role of the professional is essentially paternalistic and he seeks to protect the parent from distress, even if this reduces the information he makes available. This parent-professional relationship is essentially different from that where the child has more obvious difficulties.

> We need to think in terms of the *potentials* that a given situation has for the people in it and the *constraints* on what they can do with it. Both potentials and constraints are constructed by the history of the social relationships involved and they also change as social structures change (Connell *et al.*, op.cit., p.193)

Thus the population of parents is not necessarily homogeneous, and may be differentiated not simply by social class, but by parents' different experience of professional help. There may be as many perceptions of professional help as there are individual parents, and one particular group may not speak for all.

Parents' Partnerships with Professionals

A recent study (Sandow, Stafford and Stafford, 1987) examined the views of parents about the process of making Statements of Special Educational Need. It paid particular attention to three aspects of parental opinion which have received much attention: partnership with professionals, integration, and the choice of curriculum. It has been proposed that parents of children with problems severe enough to require a statement seek the kind of partnership described by Mittler and Mittler (1982) as

> a dialogue between parents and helpers working in partnership... Professionals have their own distinctive knowledge and skills to contribute to parents' understanding of how best to help their handicapped child, but these form a *part*, not the *whole*, of what is needed. Parents can be effective partners only if professionals take notice of what they say and of how they express their needs and treat their contribution as intrinsically important. Even where parents are unable to contribute a great deal themselves, at any rate to start with, their child's welfare will depend upon the measures recommended by professionals and can help to monitor their effects.

Similar ideas of partnerhsip with parents have been espoused by many professionals. The concept of partnership has been extended from the encouragement to parents to act as teachers or therapists for their children, to the involvement of parents in the process of making statements of special need. However, there is no real evidence that all parents of children with special needs seek this partnership, only that the most articulate appear to do so. The extrapolation of their views may do a disservice to the 'silent majority'. Sandow *et al.*, using repertory grid technique to interview parents, found that the concept of partnership was conspicuous by its absence. The term was not used by any of the 64 parents interviewed; of 24 grids completed by parents in poor socioeconomic circumstances whose children has moderate learning difficulties or emotional-behavioural difficulties, only *one* construct could be said to directly reflect partnership.

This should not really be surprising. As Moses and Croll (1987) point out,

> Parents of children with less severe educational difficulties may take the view that they have sent their children to school to be educated and that difficulties which arise at school should be resolved by the school. If parents take this view it will be very difficult for the school and other professionals to establish a relationship that could properly be called partnership.

The 'suppliers' become 'customers' by adopting consumer attitudes towards services; if one school appears unable to satisfy a child's need, it is appropriate to take him elsewhere. This is essentially the view supported by the present Secretary of State for Education and Science in respect of all children in mainstream schools. The arguments for or against such a view in general are not to be argued here – but there are particular implications for children with special educational needs, for their parents, and for the professionals with whom they deal. If parents are to be customers their view of the goods offered and of the service they receive is incompatible with any version of partnership as at present expressed. If the professionals, especially those engaged in making statements of special needs, are to become 'shopping advisers', their role, too, will change.

A second major focus of current thinking in special education is integration. Here again, parents of children with severe learning difficulties have been the main protagonists in the struggle for education in the mainstream. It has been assumed that these parents' views are typical. However, in another part of the Sandow *et al.* study, an analysis was made of the 'parental advice' proffered for the Statement. Fifty-five per cent of the 78 parents who gave advice requested placement in a special school and only 17 per cent specifically asked for placement in an ordinary school. The reasons given included the availability of a special curriculum (49 per cent), individual attention (48 per cent) and a small class or school (12 per cent). It will be interesting to see whether the advent of the new National Curriculum and periodic testing in core subjects has any effect on these preferences. Considerable anxieties have been expressed by professionals about the impact of testing on integrated children with Statements, but official responses, indicating only that such children may be exempt from some tests, have failed to take account of these concerns. It may be reasonably inferred that integration into a system where the child with special needs is excluded from the assessment (which is intended to dominate the curriculum) may make integration an even more unpopular option for parents.

We may here recall Section 10 of the 1976 Education Act, which proposed that a full curriculum, both in the classroom and in the playground, should in principle be offered to *all* children (regardless of ability) in the context of the ordinary primary or secondary school. This section was eventually repealed and superceded by the 1981 Act.

> The principle embodied in Section 10 is not new or revolutionary, but rather it accords with a consensus of public feeling that handicapped people should, so far as is possible, be enabled to take their place in the general community. (Warnock Report, paragraph 7.47)

If the full curriculum is to be defined as the new National Curriculum, it will not meet the requirements of parents as expressed in the Sandow *et al.* study. Parents' priorities were for help with communication, literacy, social and life skills. Of these, only literacy features in the National Curriculum.

If the popular view of parental priorities for partnership, integration and a full curriculum were not supported by this study, what priorities did emerge? To examine this, the parents were first asked to identify as 'elements' (that is, significant participants) those individuals (professional or otherwise) who had been involved in the assessment of their child for special education. Analysis revealed that class teachers were the most important elements in 19 cases (40 per cent of those grids in which this element was included), head teachers in 14 (28 per cent) and speech therapists in seven (25 per cent). Educational psychologists were rated most important in six cases (10 per cent). Parents' perceptions were highly role-related. The elicited constructs related to the elements were grouped into 17 categories, of which the most important was 'keeps regular contact with the child'. This contrasted with professional respondents, who saw this construct as one of the least important for parents. The seven main professional roles (doctor, teacher, head teacher, speech therapist, educational psychologist, psychiatrist, social worker) were compared with six categories of construct. These six categories were chosen from the longer list for their importance to parents, to professionals, and for their relevance to parent-professional relationships.

Table 10.1: Mean scores of seven groups of professional workers on six parental construct categories

Construct category	Child's doctor	Teacher	Head teacher	Speech therapist	Educational psychologist	Psychiatrist	Social worker
Has regular contact with child	3.83	1.5	2.65	1.87	3.88	3.45	3.11
Treats child as an individual	3.68	2.25	2.94	2.57	2.35	3.11	1.69
Sympathetic and patient with parents	2.42	2.22	2.84	1.42	2.63	3.23	2.28
Listens to parents	2.65	2.30	2.07	1.60	2.36	3.23	2.25
Keeps parents informed	2.27	2.70	2.13	1.00	3.00	2.57	3.00
Makes 'correct assessment'	3.24	2.67	2.17	2.75	2.22	3.88	3.00

Note: Lowest score = most positive perception.

From: Sandow, S., Stafford, D. and Stafford, P. (1987). *An Agreed Understanding? Parent-Professional Communication and the 1981 Education Act.* Windsor: NFER-NELSON.

The results are shown in Table 10.1. Teachers scored highest on 'has regular contact with the child' and social workers, despite scoring lowest on this category, scored highest on 'treats child as an individual' (the professionals' first priority). Speech therapists were seen as the most sympathetic and patient, as most often listening to parents and as information givers. Head teachers were seen as most likely to agree with parents on assessment, although psychologists (who did not score highly on other measures) were close behind. Doctors scored badly on almost all of these categories. Thus, parents revealed positive perceptions of those professionals whom they felt had close personal knowledge of their children. They were least approving of those who, whatever the professional expertise, were seen as remote from the 'coal face'. Problems in communication between doctors and patients have been frequently documented, for example by Ley (1977). Lipton and Svarstad (1977) describe problems of communication between doctors and parents of handicapped children: in this study, the negative perception by parents of consulting professionals was patent. In many interviews parents expressed spontaneous distrust of those who, despite their concern, could not demonstrate more than a minimal knowledge of the family, and more particularly, of the child. Partnership cannot exist without trust.

Two other factors are noteworthy. First, parents regarded the effectiveness of the professionals' relationship with the child as more important than the relationship with themselves. In other words, the focus of any encounter was the child, not the parent. Secondly the parents, although they valued regular contact with professionals, placed the *responsibility for initiating and maintaining* that contact on the professionals themselves: being 'easy to contact' was seen by parents as the least important attribute for professionals. Thus parents seemed to be seeking *support* from professionals, but not necessarily an *equal partnership*. This finding echoes that of Munn *et al.* (1982) who in a study of accountability found 'parental trust in the expertise and competence of teachers...a pervasive feature' (Munn, 1985). Munn also found that parents were only really interested in communicating with professionals on educational matters when their child was the focus of discussion.

These studies show that professional views of parental priorities may often be wide of the mark. It is natural for professionals to assume that what parents want are the skills they offer, and that the role parents wish to assume is the one defined by the professionals. Connell *et al.*'s 'potentials and constraints' apply to professionals too. This mutual construction of roles is a two-way process which is not static.

The rise of the consumer movement in education should mean that, for the first time, parental roles are being defined by parents. Many parents (particularly of children with severe learning difficulties or physical handicaps) have been active in promoting the new partnership which appears to be being offered by professionals. However, the requirements of such parents and their perception of the 'silent majority'. Furthermore, the current emphasis on 'customer accountability' may tend to foster mistrust between parents and the teachers and therapists they currently approve. This, and the emphasis on directly involving more parents in the management and organization of schools, suggests that parental roles are now being defined by politicians rather than by professionals. The potentials and constraints apply here too, of course. What evidence is there that all parents want a major role in policy making as opposed to involvement in their own child's work? There is plenty of evidence for the latter: pre-school tutoring programmes such as the *Portage Early Education Programme* (Bluma, Shearer *et al.*, 1982; Dessent, 1984), paired reading schemes (Hewison, 1985) and family support programmes (Harrison, 1981; Bell and Burn, 1979) have been characterized by enthusiastic parental support. Some parents also want to be involved in management, but in much smaller numbers. Mason (1986) found that special schools in one area had the greatest difficulty in recruiting parent governors and vacancies were filled only by extensive canvassing.

The negative perception of the consulting professionals by parents is especially worrying for those who have most influence on the 'statementing' process: the educational psychologists, psychiatrists and other medical professionals. Many (for example, Dessent, 1986) feel that the 1981 Act has forced them to return to a system where special needs are defined in terms of individual deviance rather than requisite modifications in curriculum provision. It is unlikely that the impending curricular legislation will improve the situation. Testing at seven, 11 and 14 years will emphasize the discrepancy between those who take the tests, albeit in some modified form, and those who do not. If a child with a Statement is excluded then not taking the tests will become as patent an indicator of low status as free school dinners have been. The parents of children who are experiencing problems in school, who seek individualized help and a modified curriculum (the search for which *could* lead to a kind of partnership) will be encouraged to adopt the old-fashioned and discredited view that there is something intrinsically *wrong* with their children and that it is probably *their* fault.

Chapter 11
Coordinating a Support Service

John Moore

Local education authorities vary in the way they interpret and respond to new legislation. Officers and advisers are engaged in debating intentions and directions, as well as considering the implications of reorganization and restructuring delivery services. But whatever its strategy for managing change, the local education authority must take into account the individual needs of schools and teachers, as well as those of its children. Special educational needs can only be met in a mainstream setting if teachers feel confident and well-supported. To effect this, it is important that inter-professional trust and open dialogue are promoted. Otherwise, a clear understanding of the complexities involved will be frustrated.

In practice, many local authorities have responded to recent legislation by encouraging area groups to assume responsibility and to develop appropriate initiatives. In this way, area and divisional management teams have tried to effect the necessary change by enabling professionals at grass-root level to express their views directly to those involved in decision-making.

After the Act

The law deals with the tangible, and there is nothing more tangible than a piece of paper which details how other pieces of paper should be managed. Thus, the first priority of an LEA, on receipt of an Education Act, is to ensure that all the necessary paperwork is present and correctly worded. The second priority is to ensure that deadlines for such matters as informing, collating, and issuing documents are met. Often this is sufficient to comply with the letter of the law, and there is, therefore, no further need to pursue the less tangible question, that is: 'Does the final product achieve the intention of the law?' DES-backed research, reporting in 1987, shows that as far as the 1981 Education Act is concerned, the answer is no. Whatever the intention of the law, the reality is that most LEAs spent the first two years following the enactment of the law in April 1983 developing complex paper procedures for issuing 'statements'. During the first year alone, Kent LEA wrote and issued in excess of 5,000 transitional statements. In doing so it complied with the law (each Authority was required to complete this by April 1984, though many did not), but in the process it ran up enormous waiting lists for initial assessments. This was further exacerbated in the following year by legislation requiring Mandatory Reassessments for all pupils with statements over the age of 13½ years. The pace was such that few people had the energy to consider the essential questions: 'Do these Statements reflect the real needs of the children?'; 'Do these Statements contribute to increasing parental participation, or to the development of appropriate provision?' Those who did take the trouble to ask these questions usually identified a potential as yet unrealized: 'They *could* have done, but....'

Thankfully, the development of an educational initiative does not rely on the letter of the law. It lurches, and occasionally leaps, forward by virtue of the imagination and commitment of a few individuals – be they officers, advisers, teachers or parents. It did not take too long, therefore, for the potential of the Act to be understood: that its importance lay not in the procedures for 'protecting' childrens' interests via legal statements, but in a decline in the influence of administrative procedures. In preventing decisions being made solely on the evidence of narrow and confining conditions of primary handicap, the abolition of the ten categories of handicap (which had previously dictated decisions of placement and finance and had propagated pragmatic philosophies) cleared the way for a real consideration of individual needs. To some, this was an administrative nightmare – it is easier to slot people into pigeonholes than to make a subjective assessment. That this does not seem to have been the initial intention of the legislators, is of course an irony of considerable proportion, and one which may yet give some purpose to the process of issuing Statements of need.

What follows then from an Act which has for its educational *raison d'etre* the repeal of previous Acts designed to establish provision (and, by implication, resources) for specific groups of children identified mainly on medical or quasi-medical criteria? Unfortunately, the answer must to some degree depend on the financial commitments and priorities of the LEA. Since the Act specified that the LEA must operate 'within existing resources', the onus is on the LEA to act in a morally responsible fashion. Some LEAs have protected special educational needs provision against cutbacks and have attempted to examine the resources available to them in order to reshape the provision in accordance with the 'spirit' of the Act. Some possible results of this course of action are illustrated in Figure 11.1.

Figure 11.1: Long-term repercussions of the 1981 Education Act

In April 1983 the legislation removes the ten categories of handicap, thereby removing the administrative concept of primary handicap.

↓

It is necessary to examine a wide range of contributory factors. These have to be carefully balanced so that appropriate provision can be made. Provision should reflect the individual needs of the child.

↓

Assessment techniques producing 'cut-off' criteria are no longer acceptable as necessary or suitable means of allocating places.

↓

A continuum of learning, behavioural and physical/sensory difficulties is acknowledged, based on educational assessments more closely related to actual learning needs.

↓

On accepting such a continuum, it is necessary to acknowledge a much larger group of children with special educational needs. Of particular importance are those children whose contributory problems add up to a significant learning difficulty, but who under previous assessments would not have been deemed as having a significant problem in any one area of primary handicap.

↓

continued on page 138

The move away from placement via primary handicap necessitates a view of special educational needs which more readily addresses itself to providing constructive educational answers than it does to investigating causation.

Previous and present learning experiences are included in the assessment, which leads to a profile of contributory factors. The curriculum becomes a central cause for concern.

The concept of an 'interactive' model of special educational needs is developed. Two children presenting the same degree of internal and social factors may be judged differently, one with and one without special educational needs, according to the appropriateness or otherwise of the curriculum.

The teaching of children with special educational needs becomes less associated with concepts of 'dull', 'remedial', 'slow', etc., and more associated with appropriate methods and materials. Inadequacies in teaching are highlighted: these relate to classroom management and the ability of the teacher to analyse skills and concepts.

The development of an appropriate curriculum *for all* is incorporated in a wider view of differentiation. This leads to a call for a 'whole school' approach to meeting special educational needs.

↓

Segregation, whether physical or curricular, becomes less and less tenable as new concepts appear, relating the needs of the pupil to the education on offer. These concepts carry the notion that *all* children are entitled to experience *all* elements of the curriculum; that too many pupils have been distanced from the curriculum or their peers; and that access to the curriculum means more than physical adaptations for the physically handicapped. Curriculum modification becomes a major consideration.

↓

> With more emphasis placed on the curriculum and a continuum of need, the issue of integration is widened to take in the *means* by which integration is to be achieved. The integration of the pupil is viewed increasingly as a product of the integration of levels of provision and of the integration of the personnel involved in that provision.

$$\downarrow$$

> Present provision, at all levels, must change.

The Problem of Existing Provision

As Figure 11.1 illustrates, if an LEA is to respond adequately to the challenge of decategorization, then existing forms of provision must change, some radically. This is not a question of whether they should or should not exist, but what is to be their new role. The more specialized the provision, the more difficult the answer. Paradoxically, the more types of provision, the greater the difficulty in meeting individual need. For the more provision an Authority has, the greater will be the task of integrating services and personnel.

For an Authority such as Kent, which has a wide variety of special educational needs provision, the problem of change is immense. The existence of a large number of schools for pupils with moderate learning difficulties, the divorced nature of the remedial services and tutorial units, and the distinctly separate administration of the services for the hearing impaired, present a considerable challenge. On the one hand they are a tribute to the commitment and care of the past and offer tremendous potential for the future. On the other hand they make it all too easy for the adviser, or officer, to revert to making relatively simple decisions about complex cases; or worse they may make *no* decision because the child is not yet the subject of a statement. The full Warnock 20 per cent, plus or minus, will never be satisfactorily provided for if the resources are categorized and distributed in accordance with perceived categories of need. It is extremely difficult to categorize stages of support and curriculum modification. In addition, the system of distributing resources by category leads to late intervention, since time is required for some categories to emerge; at least with sufficient evidence to confidently form the subject of a statement.

Thus the argument for prevention is weakened, since it can only be won by demonstration of proof. Whilst provision is based on category, it will be the identified (and, by implication, *severe*) cases that accrue resources. These cases may well have been identified and dealt with at an earlier, preventative stage.

The 'finger in the dyke' syndrome is all too prevalent in meeting special educational needs. A way has to be found which breaks the cycle, and decategorization would seem to offer a significant advance.

Integrating the Support Services

The first step in creating a coherent service is integration of personnel: this will allow for the devolution of resources from the predominantly exclusive use (two per cent) to wider use (20 per cent) and from late intervention to early prevention and/or support.

Integration has many levels. Functional, social and locational integration may be observed within the ordinary classroom, the ordinary school, the special school classroom, the special school, the unit, or the support service, as well as across the special/ordinary divide. So it is with integrating personnel. At one level (within the classroom) Gary Thomas (1986) describes both the difficulties and the advantages of professionals working together but performing different roles. He is careful to draw our attention to the fact that this enterprise is 'alien' to teachers, and that preparation is required to bring about maximum efficiency. Role clarification is paramount, as is in-service training which focuses on interpersonal skills. As difficult a task as this is, it is likely to prove less of a problem to the LEA than the more complex level of integrating personnel within existing support services. The same interpersonal skills and role clarification are required, but a much firmer stand needs to be taken on the question of attitudes and beliefs. A clear policy is required, and the LEA that does not communicate to its support services what its response to the 1981 Education Act is to be will simply encourage archaic practices. It will also precipitate the development of harmful rifts between those who cling to a 'category'-related services and those who wish to contribute to a more flexible view of individual needs.

It is extremely unlikely that integration of personnel, at the level of the support services, will take place without a fairly radical LEA reorganization. Such a reorganization will require a detailed analysis, area by area, of the types of services operating, how they deploy their personnel, how they organize their work, what criteria they use for prioritizing children's needs and what their current thinking is in relation to the 1981 Act. In an LEA that has some 143 units, special schools, designated schools and centres offering help to discrete groups of children, this is a formidable task. This same LEA has, since the 1981 Education Act, set up six further provisions for discrete groups of children (such as those with speech and language difficulties, problems related to dyslexia and emotional and behavioural difficulties). This fact only serves to emphasize the growing gap between the LEA's ability to provide for the wider group of children encompassed by the Act and the pressures brought about by those organizations wishing to secure greater commitment of resources to specific 'primary' disabilities – often through the vehicle of the Statement. Many LEAs may well be losing the battle, as more and more advisers and officers find their small resources eaten away by the need to find acceptable 'political' answers to these pressures. A full-scale reorganization of resources, embracing all children with special educational needs, may in the end be the only answer. Such a reorganization might be achieved in stages, each stage representing a level of integration – perhaps following the pattern of integrating personnel, buildings, material resources and then children.

The Implications for Management

Some LEAs have already realized the importance of restructuring the management of their special needs provision, and new posts have emerged which reflect a coordinating function. Within a large authority it is necessary to develop structures which allow for local initiative. To this end, the Kent LEA has taken the opportunity to develop Area Management Teams based on a general reorganization of the education service (from 14 Divisions to six Areas), a reorganization of the School Psychological Service, and a reorganization of the INSET facilities to reflect new priorities established by the Grant Related In-Service Training initiative. Drawing on the strengths and expertise of these facilities, the Area Team consists of the Area Education Officer, the Area Adviser for Special Educational Needs, the Area Senior Educational Psychologist and the Area INSET Coordinator; to be added to by a newly-proposed post – the Area Special Educational Needs Coordinator. Based on guidelines produced at County level, the Management Teams are responsible for the review and reorganization of the support services in their Area. It is this team that decides priorities and organises appropriate INSET activities at the local level.

The Area Team is vital, not only to the restructuring of provision, but also the day-to-day management of the 'integrated' service, which in the early months requires direction and moral support. It also plays an essential role during the time of negotiating a reorganization: many teachers feel threatened, and it is important that the positive aspects of the change be debated at local level. Since the reorganization leads to a new service, new roles will emerge and, by implication, a new career structure. The career structure chosen plays a vital part in both motivating the participants and managing what might otherwise by an unwieldy service. The allocation of 'integrated personnel' into Teams, to meet the needs of 'clusters' of schools, is also an essential element of this type of development.

In the case of the Kent LEA, the proposed first phase of integration is that of bringing together the Tutorial Units and Remedial Advisory Services. Both services deal with primary age children but (according to the inclination of the teacher-in-charge or the attached educational psychologist) support different (and in many cases sharply-defined) groups of children. In order to support all children with special educational needs, it is necessary to radically rethink the roles of these teachers, and in essence this is how the plan for the 'four stages of support' was conceived (see below). In addition, work carried out in primary schools to encourage a 'whole school' approach to meeting special educational needs, seemed to demand that a different approach be developed to replace that of withdrawing children from the classroom.

Four Stages of Learning Support

The model has worked well both in the primary and secondary phases. In the secondary phase, all four levels are contained within the school whereas in the primary phase, levels two, three and four are largely facilitated by the support services (formerly operating as Remedial Advisory Services, Tutorial Units and Special Schools).

Stage 1: The responsibility of the school

At Stage 1 the school, and/or subject department, is encouraged to review the methods employed and materials used, with the goal of accommodating pupils hitherto identified as presenting difficulties. The support role at this stage is confined within the secondary school to the member of department designated by the Special Needs Group and in the primary school, to the Coordinator.

Stage 2: Visiting support

At this stage, Special Needs personnel are involved. In the secondary school this is the Special Needs Department, and in the primary school, the Integrated Support Team. Their exact role is negotiated with the subject department or classroom teacher. Their roles include some of the following tasks:

a)   Advice and consultation on a wide variety of concerns.
b)   Direct support in the classroom through cooperative teaching.
c)   The Support Teacher contracts to support a school or subject department for an extended period of time, so that resources can be established and appropriate materials developed for a particular year group, band or set.
d)   The Support Teacher takes over the class, creating time for the class teacher to assess or teach individuals or small groups.

Stage 3: Withdrawal to a base

Many secondary schools operate this level of support through 'extraction' and, as previously described, most support to primary schools operates at this level. However, this form of helping pupils with special educational needs is only appropriate if it develops from Stages 1 and 2. Also, because Stage 4 deals with reintegration, it is essential that the work at the base is structured around clear objectives which are reviewed at stated time intervals (for example, half termly or termly). Teaching at this stage, therefore, bears a close relationship to the work undertaken by the teacher from whose classroom the pupil is extracted.

Base work is also used to further assess the pupil's learning needs, and the amount of time spent by any pupil at the base is dictated by individual needs; this necessitates individual timetables. The base can act as a secure area for more vulnerable pupils, who require counselling, guidance and time away from the classroom for emotional as well as learning reasons. The base within the secondary phase is the Special Needs Department. The base at the primary phase is a facility which previously operated exclusively as a Remedial Advisory Centre, Tutorial unit or Special School.

Stage 4: Reintegration

If base work is to be effective it must be followed, as quickly as possible, by phased reintegration. The support at this stage is mainly to the pupil. A timetable for reintegration is essential. The aim is to move speedily back to Stage 1. Thus, careful transfer of the support role from pupil to classroom, or department, is imperative. This aspect of the support role is quite new to those presently working in bases away from the classroom.

In time Stage 3 may be reduced in favour of Stage 2. The speed with which this happens depends largely on the attitude and the expertise of the professional involved. It could be argued that Stage 3 is either unnecessary or undesirable, as it may perpetuate inappropriate expectations on the part of the teacher or support worker. The evidence to date would point to the opposite. It would appear that a gradual transfer of resources away form a Stage 3 strategy to a Stage 2 strategy does occur, and that the very *existence* of a Stage 3 provides the stability for this change.

Clustering as a Means of Achieving an Integrated Support Service

Finally, whatever the strategy for achieving change, the LEA must take into account the individual needs of *schools* and *teachers* as well as *children*. Children's special educational needs will only be met in an integrated setting if teachers feel confident and well-supported. Teacher development is therefore of the utmost importance. This is more likely to take place if a group of schools join together under the umbrella of a local support service to share responsibility for all children with special educational needs in their geographical area. Thus the development of a Stage 3 support, whether this is at a base previously designated a Remedial Advisory Centre or a special school, should have built into it the notion of 'shared responsibility' and, wherever possible, the child should remain on the roll of his or her local ordinary school.

Clustering schools for INSET activities, particularly where the support service acts as INSET provider, is an effective way of ensuring an appropriate relationship between the supporters and the supported. It also offers the possibility of *sharing* less frequently-used and more expensive resources. More importantly, it can, if appropriately developed, offer the child a wider range of options for meeting his or her individual special educational needs, without the trauma of being removed from his or her immediate neighbourhood.

Chapter 12
Needs and Styles of In-Service Education

Neville Jones

Within a period of ten years, since the publication of the Warnock Report (1978), in-service management and courses for teachers have been under pressure to change in many (and sometimes conflicting) ways. This pressure has been due to:

- challenges about the nature of the special curriculum itself (Swann and Briggs, 1982);
- provisions in the 1981 Education Act;
- recommendations of the Advisory Committee on the Supply and Education of Teachers offering new criteria (ACSET, 1984; Sayer and Jones, 1985);
- HMI and government reports (*Better Schools*, GB.DES, 1985a; *Quality in Schools*, GB.DES, 1987; *Coping to Confidence in Further Education*, GB.DES, 1987a);
- changes in government funding to LEAs and teaching institutions.

These changes have been accompanied by a questioning of the value of in-service work carried out in traditional ways in institutions of higher education; for example, new philosophies (such as whole-school policies for management) and new principles – like integration that is related to the management of pupils with special needs in ordinary schools. Questions about *where* in-service training should take place are accompanied by questions about teaching and learning styles, and whether courses should be long- or short-term, full or part-time, comprehensive or modular. There is no longer a certainty that in-service training linked to specialist teachers of special needs constitutes a coherent body of knowledge that is separate and distinct from teacher-training and experience elsewhere in the education service. A recent slogan has asserted that *all* teachers are special needs teachers and *all* schools are special (Dessent, 1987).

The education of pupils with special educational needs in the mainstream has, in recent years, been an area subject to new ideas and leading to the promotion of new innovations. For example, the Low-Attaining Pupils Programme, came into being in July 1982 when the Secretary of State, Sir Keith Joseph, announced plans to make £2 million available for LEAs to establish projects for low-attaining pupils in fourth- and fifth-year secondary schools (GB.DES, 1986a; GB.DES, 1987; Harland and Weston, 1987).

In Oxfordshire the funding for this project was translated into three related initiatives, and retitled the New Learning Initiative (NLI). Over 1,000 pupils in 14 secondary schools became involved in a variety of courses aimed at promoting active learning and positive outcomes. The projects were also aimed at encouraging teachers to examine their perceptions of how their pupils learn through school-based in-service training and development. Pupils were encouraged to participate in the planning and assessment of their learning, with a strong emphasis on meeting individual needs, on the use of problem-solving techniques, and attaining realistic goals. This was carried out through a scheme of school community links, the appointment of school community staff, and a residential education programme. Also the introduction of a 'thinking skills' course, based on the pioneering work of Reuven Feuerstein, with theories of *Mediated Learning Experience* and techniques to improve children's thinking skills through a programme of *Instrumental Enrichment* (Sharron, 1987; Leeson, 1988). The work of instrumental enrichment in Oxfordshire has led to the designing and application of *The Oxford Skills Programme* (Hanson, 1988).

A further important change to note is the Technical and Vocational Education Initiative (TVEI) (Manpower Services Commission, 1984; GB.DES, 1985b;) with its strong grounding in module schemes for learning (Education Digest, 1986). This was in part a watershed in curriculum innovation, inspite of the political overtones in the way it was introduced and financed, and for some educationalists might well be 'the most important event in secondary education since Circular 10/65' (Dancy, 1984). This view is countered by those who view the introduction of TVEI as part of the government's programme towards centralization, which aims to realign education towards the needs of industry and the economy and to introduce elements of learning not compatible with principles of comprehensiveness in secondary education (McMurray, 1987). Not only will TVEI be part of the curriculum in secondary education, but the programme will be funded by the government for substantial expansion (GB.DES, 1986b). It is not clear how an innovation like TVEI fits in comfortably with ideas about student choice in education and student-led interest curricula. Perhaps this is but one paradox in current educational practice, that freedom to learn (like parent choice), is only a freedom to select from a range of predetermined options ordained by government. Thirdly, changes are coming into existence nationally through schemes of 'records of achievement' (GB.DES, 1984a), 'pupils profiling', and with LEA consortia working on curricula schemes like the Oxford Certificate of Educational Achievement (Brighouse, 1982, 1985; Wakefield, 1985).

At the time of writing, the government has published its proposals for a new Education Reform Bill with provision for a national curriculum linked to a system of 'bench-mark' testing for pupils at regular stages in their school careers, changes in the way schools are to be financed, a facility for schools to 'opt out' of local authority control and parents to have a wider choice of schools for their children. The thrust towards a national curriculum arises from a view that any curriculum must be both broad and balanced: in many schools, at fourth- and fifth-year level, the core is very small and the optional curriculum elaborate. If there is a consensus view that a national curriculum is necessary, this is balanced with much dispute as to the nature of the subject and the amount of time given over to the core syllabus. Nowhere in the government's proposals for a national core curriculum does there seem to be an acknowledgement of the considerable amount of work teachers have carried out to develop appropriate curriculum policies and programmes for all who attend school, irrespective of measured ability and need. Nor, for that matter, is there any acknowledgement of new approaches to learning with *the student* central to setting personal goals and objectives. Possibly because there has been too much disagreement among educationalists about the aims and content of education and the curriculum (let alone the learning styles and approaches to be adopted) this has produced a backlash from parents which a centralizing government has capitalized upon. A consequence of the new Education Bill is that at least an additional 175 powers for control have been created for exercise by the Minister of Education.

The implications for in-service needs of teachers arising from legislation has yet to be determined. Of particular concern to those who work with pupils who have special needs is what will happen to pupils with such needs as a result of 'bench-mark' testing of pupils at seven, 11, 14 and 16 years of age. A further cause for concern is parents' choice about schools: the only criterion for parents to make their choices may be the national examination results, which (for the most part) are not related to the bottom 40 per cent of the ability spectrum. There is no originality in 'bench-mark' mentality but the political motivation has changed: a century ago there were pronouncements about educational aims and objectives which today again find a place in educational thinking.

Styles of Delivery

For the purpose of this chapter, and issues related, we can consider three main styles of in-service work, some of which is still both innovatory and exploratory. Firstly, there are many variations, introducing flexible ways of working on course work, now taking place in relation to *'institutional' in-service* (that is, work related to institutions of higher education). Secondly, we can look at *whole-school approaches* to school management and the implications this has for in-service work. Thirdly, we may consider an account of *distance learning* where this has been pioneered in Britain, as for example, in the field of special educational needs at the Open University.

(a) Institutional in-service training

Changes that have taken place in government funding for teacher in-service training, and increasing limitations on resources, have encouraged more flexible ways whereby teachers may acquire higher or specialist qualifications. Davies (1988), in a personal communication, has listed the range of delivery system as follows:

- Conventional one-year full-time secondments provided by institutions of higher education;
- One term full-time secondment similar to the present SENIOS courses;
- Range of part-time provision one-day a week over a period of a term or a year;
- Exchange placements between teachers and other professionals in different forms of schools and institutions;
- Distance learning packages;
- Associateships to colleges of higher education.

Davies has also drawn attention to the fact that one-year full-time courses are likely to give way to a system of awards that will allow students to accumulate a credit bank, through modular types of study. A modular system of learning is now becoming common-place in schools, although the evidence for its implementation is still somewhat impressionistic. Some data has been compiled arising from surveys carried out by the School Curriculum Development Committee (SCDC) during 1985/6 in comprehensive schools, grammar and secondary modern, single-sex and mixed schools, sixth form colleges, community colleges and middle schools (Watkins, 1986). These surveys indicated that:

- over half of all LEAs are involved in the development of modular elements in the school curriculum – in some LEAs modular development is now part of an authority's policy for its secondary school curriculum;
- over a third of all LEAs have designated an administrator, usually a senior advisor, to facilitate the development of modular courses;
- if there has been a single substantial impetus for modularizing the curriculum then this has come through the Technical, Vocational and Education Initiative (TVEI) programme.

Modular curriculum development in Oxfordshire schools is being developed through the Oxfordshire Examination Syndicate (OES). This is a major collaborative scheme, linked with the Southern Examining Group (SEG), whereby a consortium of schools and colleges in the County administer a bank for GCSE credits. This means that the SEG is committed to working in an open and flexible partnership with the Oxfordshire Examining Syndicate, thus ensuring that 'curriculum assessment and teaching methods develop in harmony, and avoiding situations where syllabuses designed away from classrooms dictate educational objectives and methods'. The Southern Examining Board is available to the Syndicate for consultation and assistance at an early stage in the design of credits, and has rearranged its administrative procedures to accommodate the system of credit banking. Modular schemes are now being introduced by a number of teaching institutions providing modular courses for the study of special educational needs (Robson, 1984), much of which has developed from the modular style of learning for special needs promoted by the Open University in 1982 and described elsewhere in this chapter (see page 159).

Hodgson and Trotter (1988) discount the 'single package' approach to in-service training and advocate 'three interconnected phases, involving several parties to the participating teachers'. First, there is a need for a school, the LEA, and the institution providing the in-service training, to carry out a situational analysis of the nature of the problems in each of the different schools participating. This would entail nominating key members of staff who would have a responsibility to manage tasks relating to the provision of special needs provision. The main tasks would be that of prioritizing and specifying goals for the schools, and linking these to the actual courses: senior school management would be expected to make a commitment to support this work and to ensure appropriate follow-through in the post in-service period.

In the second phase, whether part- or full-time, the course itself should address the following:

- Participants working on their own identified tasks and goals. The aim here is to secure 'ownership' for the participating teachers processed through a programme of 'action-learning' (Revans, 1980).
- The context of the in-service course must be in a format that aligns itself with 'action-learning' proposals. A particular in-service course will not, therefore, be a static programme but will change each year according to (a) topics identified in the participating schools; and (b) topics which in themselves facilitate the 'action-learning' process.

The task of deciding and negotiating which tasks are to be responded to, and in what format, will be that of the staff providing the in-service course. Hodgson and Trotter, however, suggest that in any in-service course there would be the need to cover a number of issues which they list as follows:

- school and classroom organization;
- resource allocation;
- curriculum modification;
- monitoring pupil progress;
- parent participation in their child's educational progress;
- parental rights in the assessment procedures;
- development of staff support from outside the school.

All these aspects arise from recent legislation related to in-service practice in ordinary schools.

A second issue is that of self-management, which is receiving increasing attention by the trainers (Pedler and Boydell, 1985) and psychologists engaged with helping teachers to cope with their day-to-day stresses (Dunham, 1986, 1988). Thirdly, there is the area of problem-solving, which is related not so much to individual pupil thinking and learning as to solving day-to-day management of the task identified by teachers who participate in in-service work (Taylor, 1985; Jackson, 1985). A fourth area is that of communication among the networks of teachers and parents, and support agencies, for establishing and maintaining mutual support and cooperation in both designing and carrying out curricular innovation and practice. This task is aided by the literature on management cooperation and simulation work.

By this stage the in-service participants, in cooperation with the trainers, will have identified the tasks and areas which might legitimately be covered by a course of in-service work, have decided on the strategies necessary to explore the tasks within an 'action-learning' format, and be engaged in the process of the in-service programme. This then leads to the third and final stage: the implementation of the knowledge and strategies learned on the in-service course. It is here that Hodgson and Trotter (1988) see a shift in the focus of the ownership: away from the training institution and back to the context of the participant's own schools. The responsibility of the training staff is not abandoned here, although this is characteristic of many in-service courses. The trainers would follow-up and visit the schools 'to assist in the clarification and implementation' of the solutions worked out for the originally identified tasks. Within an LEA it might also be anticipated that those following the in-service course might, with benefit, continue to work together in a need for work of professional cooperation (visiting each other's schools, for example, and meeting possibly once a term to compare progress). The activity might then be coupled with later reference back to the training institution using the in-service staff as a 'resource' for future development.

(b)   Whole-school and local contexts

Sayer (1985) has drawn attention to how ACSET tried to plan a full training programme for diversity in schools, whereby the needs of teachers can be met at different local situations, with these changing according to circumstance. One model of local implementation is the whole-school approach, which in itself posed certain problems as these related to special educational needs. Sayer pinpoints a problem central to the management of needs in ordinary schools and one which in outcome affects all other aspects of school management whether for special needs or not. This is the continuing practice of treating special needs as a separate management entity within ordinary schools: separate for resource allocation, teacher training, pupil grouping, and so forth, all this a 'result of outmoded and discredited attitudes towards handicap and the handicapped'. The logic of this is that if we combine, say, two aspects of current thinking about how ordinary schools should be managed, a whole-school approach combined with a philosophy of integration of the disabled, then we stop referring to pupils as 'special' and we cease to run 'special' initial and in-service training courses. In-service, in a whole-school context, means that we 'normalize' and do not 'marginalize', any individual pupil or group with disabilities. There is simply a recognition that in schools there is a diversity of normal needs which have to be met. It is to normal in-service budgets and post-professional training that we should look for funding and the acquisition of knowledge and skills to meet these needs of pupils.

As well as identifying the main point of principle, Sayer draws attention to some of the present problems related to the development of teachers' skills in ordinary schools for meeting the needs of pupils referred to as 'special'.

- Little expert resource from outside the school, as for example, from educational psychologists, in relation to curriculum issues.
- The largely irrelevant experience of special school teachers, skilled in teaching in the special environments of special schools and units, to offer advice and support to management of special needs in ordinary classrooms.
- The continued use of individual testing and assessment by support teachers and psychologists, through tools that assume a mythological national norm. This is of limited use for classroom teachers in adapting the curriculum to meet individual needs.

Sayer notes that confusions about special needs, and pupils with such needs in ordinary schools, are exemplified both in the Warnock Report and the 1981 Education Act. Special education is a system of 'exceptional' management, having it sown criteria for selection of pupils, building, staff training, financing. The Warnock Committee acknowledged the *principle* of integration, but then described those categories of pupils who would still need to be placed in the segregated 'exceptional' system. Integration would be a simple transfer arrangement so that 'exceptional' management would be transferred geographically onto the sites of ordinary schools with little or no change in approach or attitudes to the disabled. Within ordinary schools we have considered special on-site classes or departments to be used during a traditional period between total segregation and total integration specialist staff and a specialist support system to ordinary teachers. Whatever gains there might be in having the 'exceptional' system located within ordinary schools, the danger remains that the new school management to evolve may simply be one of ordinary education with a built-in, self-contained (and self-perpetuating) special education system.

This is what has happened in many LEAs, and this shift-without-change in the management of special educational needs, has been underpinned by the provision of the 1981 Education Act and the DES recategorization of pupils with moderate learning needs. For a number of LEAs the action has been to relocate personnel and redirect financial resources under a pretence of following an integration policy. Hence, there has been some limitation on resources put into integrated special education, but a massive build-up of services (now referred to by a variety of titles, such as 'special needs advisory teacher services') and a clear demarcation of special facilities within the ordinary schools. Is this the system within which teachers working in ordinary schools, ordinary and special education, have to work and address their in-service needs? In such schools, where special needs are so clearly demarcated it is not clear whether in-service training for special needs is for teachers working with 'normal' groups of pupils, or specialist teachers working in the on-site units, classes and special departments.

The issue becomes even more blurred when attempts are made to 'integrate' the special unit pupils, for part of their education, in the ordinary classes. Teachers working in the mainstream soon discover that the resources to help pupils from the LEA special needs budget are directed into the 'special' aspects of ordinary school management without any guarantee that this will be beneficial to pupils in the mainstream of the school. When requests are made to the LEA administration for extra help with a pupil in ordinary lessons, then the LEA response is that the school is already resourced for its special needs pupils. In outcome this means that any pupils' need has to be subjected to the time-consuming and irrelevant administrative procedures of the 'statementing' practices perpetrated as a consequence of the 1981 Education Act. Pupils have to become 'special' to receive help for needs which, prior to the 1981 Act, were part of the spectrum of the diversity of ordinary needs in ordinary schools!

Changes in the way we manage schools when whole-school policies become operative have been identified by Sayer. Some of the issues may be summarized as follows:

a) *Appropriate curriculum*
   The response to pupils with special educational needs is not just within the framework of the formal curriculum: pupils with special needs also have needs in the wide range of non-curricular activities in the school, the extra-curricula, and indeed, the hidden curricula of a pupil's time at school.

b) *Integrating 'support' services*
   Integration is not just a concept for school management. It must find reflection in the way all services, interlinked, work to make the education service effective. Questionable is the

value of support services that function peripatetically. It makes even less sense to have an LEA administration for mainstream education and a separate officer service for special needs.

c) *Phasing out educational phase structures*
Whatever the problems posed for pupils moving from one phase in education to another (requiring enormous personal adjustments for some pupils), the problems are even more compounded for pupils with special needs. If there is a case to be argued for a more gradual evaluation in the learning process, from the whole-curriculum style of the primary school to the subject-orientated approach of secondary education, then this would entail a move away from separate infant, primary, middle and secondary schools. Natural breaks at ages five, eight and 11 years (which for most pupils are *unnatural*) would be a thing of the past.

d) *Styles of learning*
A school curriculum has to be a fused system of what currently happens as part of the core curricula, extra-curriculum activities, and elements of the hidden curricula. This is simply the sum total of what pupils do while they are at school. The overall need is for appropriate curricula to suit individual needs in all aspects of growing and learning from five to 16 years. Flexibility in course work and class size are also changes that are part of whole-school management. It is not just a question of all pupils having equal access to the full range of subjects and experiences available; it is also necessary to consider the structure of *how* the learning can take place. Group size has to be matched with subject to be learned. This means that pupils may learn some areas of the curriculum alone, in quiet, directing their own work and using teachers only as a resource. Some learning can be in very large groups, far higher than the nominal groups of 30 often seen in classrooms today. Learning has to be towards short-term goals that can be assessed, that will allow regular reappraisal of the directions for learning being followed, and for changes to be made. The advent of modular curricula makes much of this possible. For many pupils with special educational

needs modular styles of learning provide the breakthrough that is needed.

e) *Community education*

As many schools begin to embrace the 'community' approach to their work, this brings with it new dimensions for mainstream teachers – as well as for those directly concerned with special educational needs. Home-school links are becoming more of a reality through greater parent participation on school governing bodies, and in helping with their children's learning (Morgan, 1988). The open evening for parents, who queue up for 'interviews', is gradually giving way to more informal teacher-pupil contact. It may be that the traditional 'parent-teacher' association of a school will give way to a new kind of grouping for learning purposes, for example a member of staff working with a small group of parents *and their children* together, with the emergence of a group and a team spirit for the benefit of all those concerned. It may be the case that the greatest need for teachers over the next few years is in developing appropriate skills in working with parents individually and in small groups: thus involving not just form teachers but all who work in schools. This would then be the in-service need requiring acknowledgement and action for funding. Sayer (1985a) has called these teacher-parents-pupils groupings as 'cells having meaning for everyone'.

f) *Whole-school management*

Sayer (1985a), in *What Future for Secondary Schools*, writes: 'Schools contribute to a whole curriculum; the school curriculum by itself cannot be considered whole; to have sense and validity, schools must work in context, of the learning experience at home, through media, and in the local community...'

'If the school becomes a family and neighbourhood resource rather than just an institution in which to place children of a particular age, then it is also more likely to be acceptable to those with special educational needs, and to respond flexibly.'

'There will still be concerns for a broad, balanced and relevant curriculum which includes or is completed by schools; but to discover that schools, parents and others in the locality have to work together and plan together with young learners. That demands a different kind of teacher, a different set of relationships, and a different kind of training.'

'Schools ought to become multiprofessional, starting with the integration of specific professional services within the education business (Jones and Sayer, 1988). Educational social workers, counsellors, career officers, educational psychologists, peripatetic remedial and multicultural services, ought to be part of the same show.'

'Alternative education, now too often expressed in off-site sanctuaries, shelters, or sin-bins, should be part of the same mainstream service, recognized and supported from within – teachers and specific professionals have to learn to work together, not by referral and chain reaction, but in concert under the same management.'

'Nowhere more than in providing for children with special educational needs is it apparent that a school framework based on year-groups and age-bands is inappropriate. A continuum of response across age sectors is more important a notion than a continuum of response across the bands of specific, or integration and segregation. That may mean facing the fact that current divisions between primary, secondary and further education, or between these and various forms of youth and community or adult and continuing education are artificial, limiting, and unnecessary for more than specific purposes. We may have to move away from the current government insistence on training teachers for specific ages, and look towards a local federation of education services and the ability of teachers to stretch the system and themselves.'

(c) Distance learning: the Open University

In 1982 the Open University offered to students its first full course on the education of handicapped children. The course, E241 *Special*

Needs in Education, available in both the undergraduate and associate student programmes, provided a general introduction to the field of special needs utilizing a range of disciplines: psychology, sociology, economics, history and politics. The course themes are such that groups other than teachers in ordinary and special education can find an interest where there is an interest in the education needs of children and young people. The main themes are:

- Understanding what special education is like and what it entails to be a participant.
- Meeting the special needs of children in education, the gaps in the services and why they exist, and the ways forward for a better educational service for a substantial number of pupils with designated special needs.
- How special education relates to the LEA system of education as a whole, the different styles of response to special needs in ordinary schools, and where there is an interaction between the special segregated system and mainstream education.
- The conditions for successfully integrating pupils with special educational needs into ordinary schools, why they were segregated in the first instance, and the problems of creating a climate for the changes needed so that the integration can occur.

The courses on distance learning related to special educational needs raise a number of questions about distance learning in general. This can first be looked at by simply asking the question 'how do students learn at a distance'? Already there are substantial theories about learning in classrooms, with face-to-face interaction between teacher and learner (Bruner, 1966). It may be postulated that we could consider theories are implicit in the learning taking place at a distance. Distance learning is about use of the media, mainly television, the provision of tutorial time (that is the amount of face-to-face teaching and seminar work necessary to supplement or make effective what is taught at a distance) and the nature of learning material itself (units and set books, project work, style of television presentation).

Research into these areas has been summarized by Perraton (1987). A study of Trenaman (1967), comparing the presentation of information through media resources of radio, television and publications, and comparing those with learning by other occupation groups of students, showed that learning was determined more by virtue of the occupational group than by virtue of differences in media presentation. In other words, 'communications media do not differ in their educational effectiveness'. The issue here appears to be one of student choice for their own individualized methods of learning and that learning can only be maximized when students have a real choice about this rather than a contrived choice where they have to decide between full-, short-, part-time, institutional, school-based or distance learning. Balanced against this is a view, with as yet little empirical evidence, that students have a higher completion rate for their courses if distance teaching utilizes a combination of media techniques.

Possibly this depends on the uptake of different methods by individual students. Certainly, the basis of much of the work carried out by the Open University, and presumably by the Open College, will on the premise that 'the practical advantages of combining broadcasting with print and with face-to-face learning' ... 'lie in the power of broadcasts to stimulate, the power of face-to-face tutoring to relate subject matter to individual response, and the power of print to give permanence' (Perraton, 1987, p.5).

Possibly a major difficulty with distance learning is where a choice of style for individual learning masks an inability, or just lack of confidence, to cope with new learning. All too often this has its roots in a student's past, usually childhood experience of failed learning at school. Sometimes the flexible structure of distance learning allows such a student to pace the new learning at a rate suited to the student's emotional and psychological needs in relation to learning, and for the student to control his or her own stress. This places a special responsibility on local tutors to be aware when a student is adopting positive stances to anxiety about learning, and doing something positive about it, and when student isolation is self-defeating. The face-to-face tutorial provides, as Perraton has listed, some five functions, all of which facilitate effective learning for the student and effective feedback for the tutor:

- the opportunity for personal encouragement;
- the correction of errors in prepared material;
- to alert tutors to student learning difficulties;
- to provide feedback for those preparing materials;

- to allow for individualization in learning responses that are the essence of dialogue between teacher and those taught (Peters, 1972; Freire, 1972).

While all these aspects of the learning process are operating in face-to-face learning contexts, the types of interaction listed and the modes of feedback, have to be managed differently in situations where distance learning is the major mode for communication with the student, or where this is the student's choice. The question for every Open University tutor (and this applies with even more force in special needs courses, where attitudes and prejudices are central issues to understanding society's policies and practices) is how far face-to-face tutoring has to be maximized for individual students, or corporately, in order to increase the effectiveness of education provided within a distance teaching paradigm. It is at this stage, that distance learning and its specific priorities for techniques like face-to-face tutoring, have to be balanced with other forms of service delivery, according to whether particular procedures are cost-effective.

Perraton, in his article, also looks at the design of instructional material, the question of administration of the system and how we go about the assessment task. Trenaman (1967) claims that understanding is improved where material is personalized, dramatic, and in the form of a story. Also, that learning with radio is increased if the broadcaster provides the listener with the answers in the same programme that the questions are posed (Galton and Serle, 1980). Many institutions involved in distance learning facilitate their course material by providing course guides. In course E806 on *Applied Studies in Learning Difficulties in Education*, students are provided with a project guide describing for students 'a variety of methods of collecting and interpreting information', aimed at helping them with their three research projects. The main function of the Guide is to ensure that in following through research methodology the students do not lose sight of the issues related to special needs that underpin the projects (Potts, 1987). Also for this course there is a set of Tutor Notes and a study guide for tutors and a Guide to an Active Learning Pack EP 538 written by Potts and Booth (see Potts, 1983), both members of the E806 Course team. From the research literature, and an analysis of course guides, Perraton derived three propositions about student needs when they learn away from a student group or from teaching in face-to-face contexts:

- learning increases when there are advance indicators in the text;
- students find the texts more accessible when they are written utilizing the first and second person (rather than third person) and the active (rather than passive) voice;
- there is an increase in learning when subject material is structured in a coherent way, taking account of the student's previous learning.

These statements, used to specify methods and styles of learning and linked to distance learning technqiues, say very little about the process of 'learning' itself. There have been many theories about this with the result that much distance education has concentrated on aspects of training and instruction. Balanced with this are those aspects which Stenhouse (1975) has called 'initiation' (that is, students being initiated into social norms) and 'induction' (a process of introducing students to systems of thinking that can lead to making judgements).

Assessment of distance learning raises questions of whether a particular course is worthwhile, a value judgement, and the methods to be employed to assess the qualities that the course sets out to import, a qualification process. It is not always easy, even when desirable, to equate quality issues with quantifiable variables. It is not an uncommon complaint of students that a final examination for a course is not only irrelevant, but trivializes the previous learning, especially when the structure of the course material provides within itself a form of continuous assessment. Here we are often caught up in a dialectical dilemma, balancing on the one hand the value of course work for students who may wish to apply their learning to very *practical situations* (as with teachers in their teaching) and on the other hand discussions about the value of courses to some *larger set of objectives* related more to the value systems of a given society, and how these are projected and sustained to ensure their continuity among the population.

Discussion

The changes in ideology, structural management, and facilities for in-service work, some of which have been described above, have brought about a diversity compounded by confusion in relation to how in-service training might develop over the next few years. To bring about a 'more systematic and purposeful planning of in-service training' the government, through its 'grant-related in-service training for teachers' programme (GRIST), has attempted to introduce more structure into the system. The new system for awarding grants was foreshadowed in DES Circular 6/86 (GB.DES, 1986a). What was envisaged by the government in its GRIST arrangements was that LEAs would restructure their in-service management in ways that would be consistent with the new style of funding. In some LEAs this happened, with new management structures linked to effective schemes for staff development. Elsewhere, LEAs have attempted to 'graft the new arrangements onto a traditional system', and they are now having to cope, and finance, substantial increases in bureaucratic management, with increasing complexity of organization. A consequence of this is that 'the administration involved in the identification of teacher's needs, the required monitoring and evaluation of INSET, the process of budgeting and bidding for grants, and the liaison with providers, has in some instances diverted funds into the management of INSET rather than into provision for teachers' (Jones and Reid, 1987).

In some LEAs, through either management naïveté or just inability to cope managerially with change, there have been complete new in-service departments established, carrying out work previously covered effectively by area educational officers. It is not surprising, therefore, that when changes for better and improved educational services are responded to with substantial increases in bureaucracy (usually at the expense of teachers and their schools) the government is anxious to place financial management more in the hands of schools. Other changes seem to be taking place because of the Government's new funding arrangements. Some of these are simply a response to central government rate-capping, but others are due to the removal of the 'pool' whereby a local authority could recoup 75 per cent of the cost of paying a supply teacher to provide cover while the teacher is on secondment. LEAs having a large number of small and rural schools may well have to reduce the opportunities for staff from such schools to take full-time secondments. If the answer here is to promote school based in-service work, the differences between increasing individual professional skills and those that benefit the school at large, and the interrelationship of these two aspects, have to be carefully worked out. There is then the question of priorities: the needs of the teachers, the school, the LEA and those of central government.

Jones and Reid (1987) point out that many primary school head-teachers are over-burdened because of:

- extra demands imposed by new contracts;
- devolution of finance control;
- fluctuating pupil rolls;
- changes in the composition and power of governing bodies;

and that teacher-training institutions have now to cope with:

- sudden shrinkage in the numbers of full-time students;
- shifts from long-term courses to those that are short, sharp, school-focused and skills-orientated.

From some preliminary research work carried out at Exeter University by Professor Ted Wragg it has been shown that there has been a significant drop in the numbers of teachers attending full-time, one-year in-service courses. This was a predictable forecast that many concerned with teacher training were able to make when the government first suggested that LEAs should have more freedom to spend their in-service money as they wished (Mittler, 1986). In terms of numbers attending, the survey showed that there had been a fall from 2,112 teachers on full-time secondments in 1986 to 673 in 1987. The demand now is for short non-award bearing courses. One effect of these changes is to push in-service work even further towards modular styles, and also to produce arrangements whereby teachers wanting to secure higher degree qualifications are able to do so by possibly selecting a range of module courses from a variety of sources, from higher and further education institutions, as well as from module courses that have been developed by LEAs. In this way we may see all who have left school embarking on a system of obtaining module credits which they can then credit to their personal educational bank, linking these to accredited diplomas and degrees and doing so throughout their lives.

References

ASSOCIATION OF EDUCATIONAL PSYCHOLOGISTS (1987). Changes in Establishments of LEA Psychological Services since 1981. *Circular to Principal Educational Psychologists*, 9.4.87.

BAILEY, T.J. (1981). 'The secondary remedial teacher's role redefined', *Remedial Education*, 16, 3, 132-136.

BALSHAW, M. (1987). 'Mainstreaming support work – what *is* it all about?' In: BOWERS, T. (Ed.) *Special Educational Needs and Human Resource Management*. London: Croom Helm.

BARNSLEY SPECIAL EDUCATION TEAM. (1981). 'A team approach to disruption', *Special Education, Forward Trends*, 8, 1.

BARTON, L. and TOMLINSON, S. (Eds) (1984). *Special Education and Social Interests*. London: Croom Helm.

BELL, S. and BURN, C. (1976). *A Kind of Challenge: The Story of Liverpool Home-link*. 54, Brittarge Brow, Liverpool 27.

BETTELHEIM, B. and ZELAN, K. (1982). *On Learning to Read*. London: Thames and Hudson.

BETTELHEIM, B. (1988). *A Good Enough Parent*. London: Thames and Hudson.

BINES, H. (1986). *Redefining Remedial Education*. London: Croom Helm.

BINES, H. (1988). 'Equality, community and individualism: The development and implementation of the whole school approach to special educational needs'. In: BARTON, L. (Ed.) *The Politics of Special Needs*. Lewes: Falmer Press.

BLAU, P.M. (1964). *Exchange and Power in Social Life*. London: Wiley.

BLUMA, S., SHEARER, M., FROHMAN, A. and HILLIARD, J. with WHITE, M. and CAMERON, S. (1987). *The Portage Early Education Programme*. Windsor: NFER-NELSON.

BOOTH, T.A. (1978). 'From normal baby to handicapped child: unravelling the idea of subnormality in families of mentally handicapped children', *Sociology* 12, 203-21.

BOOTH, T. (1981). 'Demonstrating integration'. In: SWANN, W. (Ed.) *The Practice of Special Education*. Oxford: Blackwell.

BOWERS, T. (1987). *Special Educational Needs and Human Resource Management*. London: Croom Helm.

BRIGHOUSE, T.R.P. (1982). *Making Schools Fit for Teachers and Teachers Fit for Schools*, Paper read to the Centre for the Study of Comprehensive Schools. York, July.

BRIGHOUSE, T.R.P. (1985). 'OCEA: 16- to 18-year-olds', *Local Government Policy Making*, July.

BROCK, M. (1976). 'The Problem Family', *Child: Care, Health and Development*, 2, 39-43.

BRONFENBRENNER, U. (1979). *The Ecology of Human Development*. Cambridge, Mass.: Harvard University Press.

BRUNER, J.S. (1966). *Towards a Theory of Instruction*. Cambridge: Cambridge University Press.

BRUNER, J. (1974). *The Relevance of Education*. London: Penguin.

BURDEN, R. (1973). 'If we throw tests out of the window what is there left to do?' *Journal of the Association of Educational Psychologists*. 3, 6-9.

BUTT, N. (1986). 'Implementing the whole school approach at secondary level', *Support for Learning*, 1, 4, 10-15.

CAMERON, R.J. (1982). *Working Together: Portage in the U.K.* Windsor: NFER-NELSON.

CLARKE, T. and WATKINS, S. (1983). Ski-Hi Home Intervention Program. Department of Communication Disorders Utah State university.

CLUNIES-ROSS, L. and WIMHURST, S. (1983). *The Right Balance: Provision for Slow Learners in Secondary Schools*. Windsor: NFER-NELSON.

CONNELL, R.W., ASHENDEN, D.J., KESSLER, S. and DOWSETT, G.W. (1982). *Making the Difference: Schools, families and social division*. Australia: Allen and Unwin.

CONWAY, J.M. (1987). An ethnographic study of special educational needs decision making in a Local Education Authority Office. Unpublished by M.Ed dissertion.

CONWAY, J.M. and HEPWORTH, R. (1987). 'Barnsley responds to the 1981 Act', *British Journal of Special Education*, 14, 2, 54-57.

COTTON, E. Basic Motor Pattern.

COULBY, D. (1986). 'Intervening in classrooms'. *Association of Child Psychology and Psychiatry* 8, 1.

COX, D. (1987). A survey of Speech Therapy services for children with particular reference to special education. A report for *Voluntary Organizations Communication and Language*. London: South Western Hospital.

CRYSTAL, D., FLETCHER, P. and GERMAN, M. (1978). *The Grammatical Analysis of Language Disability*. London: Edward Arnold.

CRYSTAL, D. (1982). *Profiling Linguistic Disability*. London: Edward Arnold.

DANCY, J. (1984). 'TVEI', Editorial Introduction to the University of Exeter Publication *TVEI: Perspectives 14*, School of Education: University of Exeter.

DANIEL, E. (1984). 'A suggested model of remedial provision in a comprehensive school', *Remedial Education*, 19,2,78-83.

DAVIES, J.D. and DAVIES, P. (1988). 'Developing credibility as an advisory and support teacher', *Support for Learning* 3,1,12-15.

DAVIES, J.D. (1988). Personal Communication. School of Education, Oxford Polytechnic.

DESSENT, T. (1984). 'Special schools and the mainstream – "The resource stretch"'. In: BOWERS, T. (Ed.) *Management and the Special School*. London: Croom Helm.

DESSENT, T. (1985). 'Supporting the mainstream: do we know how?' *Education and Child Psychology*. 2,3.

DESSENT, T. (1986). 'Educational Psychologists and the Act', *Policy and Provision for Special Needs Newsletter*. London: Institute of Education.

DESSENT, T. (1987). *Making the Ordinary School Special*. Basingstoke: Falmer Press.

DONALDSON, M. (1978). *Children's Minds*. Glasgow: Fontana/Collins.

DUNHAM, J. (1986). *Stress in Teaching*, Beckenham: Croom Helm.

DUNHAM, J. (1988). 'Stress in teaching'. In: JONES, N.J. (Ed.) *Special Educational Needs Yearbook, 1*. London: Frank Cass.

DYER, C. (1988). 'Which support ?: an examination of the term', *Support for Learning*, 3,1,6-11.

EDUCATION DIGEST (1986). 'The TVEI Programme: past, present and future', *Journal of Education*, 19 September.

EVANS, J. (1985). *Teaching in Transition: the Challenge of Mixed Ability Groupings*. London: Longman.

EDWARDS, C. (1985). 'On launching a support service', *British Journal of Special Education*, 12,2,53-54.

EMERICK, L. and HATTEN, J. (1979). *Diagnosis and Evaluation in Speech Pathology*. London: Prentice-Hall.

FERGUSON, N. and ADAMS, M. (1982). 'Assessing the advantages of team teaching in remedial education: the remedial teacher's role', *Remedial Education*, 7,1.

FISH, J. (1985a). *Special Education: The Way Ahead*. Milton Keynes: Open University Press.

FISH, J. (1985b). *Educational Opportunities for All* (The Fish Report).

FREIDSON, E. (1973). *The Professions and Their Prospects*. London: Sage Publications.

FREIRE, P. (1972). *Pedagogy of the Oppressed*. Harmondsworth: Penguin.

GALLOWAY, D. and GOODWIN, C. (1987). *The Education of Disturbing Children*. London: Longman.

GALTON, K. and SEARLE, B. (1980). *The Radio Mathematics Project. Introduction and Guide.* Stanford: Institute for Mathematical Studies in the Social Sciences.

GATH, A. (1972). 'The effect of mental subnormality on the family', *British Journal of Hospital Medicine*, August.

GILLHAM, B. (1978). *Reconstructing Educational Psychology.* London: Croom Helm.

GIPPS, C. and GOLDSTEIN, H. (1984). 'More than a change in name?'. *Special Education, Forward Trends*, 11,4,6-8.

GIPPS, C., GROSS, H. and GOLDSTEIN, H. (1987). *Warnock's Eighteen Per Cent: Children With Special Needs in Primary Schools.* Lewes: Falmer Press.

GLENDINNING, C. (1983). *Unshared Care: parents and their disabled children.* London: Routledge and Kegan Paul.

GOACHER, B., EVANS, J., WELTON, J. and WEDELL, K. (1987). *The 1981 Education Act: Policy and Provision for Special Educational Needs.* London: Cassell.

GOLBY, M. and GULLIVER, R.J. (1979). 'Whose remedies, whose ills? – A critical review of remedial education', *Journal of Curriculum Studies*, 11.

GOODWIN, C. (1983). 'The contribution of support services to integration policy'. In: BOOTH, T. and POTTS, P. (Eds) *Integrating Special Education.* Oxford: Blackwell.

GREAT BRITAIN. DEPARTMENT OF EDUCATION AND SCIENCE (1975). Circular 2/75. *The Discovery of Children Requiring Special Education and the Assessment of their Needs.* London: HMSO.

GREAT BRITAIN. DEPARTMENT OF EDUCATION AND SCIENCE (1981). *Education Act 1981.* London: HMSO.

GREAT BRITAIN. DEPARTMENT OF EDUCATION AND SCIENCE (1984a). *Records of Achievement: A Statement of Policy.* London: HMSO.

GREAT BRITAIN. DEPARTMENT OF EDUCATION AND SCIENCE (1984b). *Slow Learning and Less Successful Pupils in Secondary Schools.* London: HMSO.

GREAT BRITAIN. DEPARTMENT OF EDUCATION AND SCIENCE (1984c). ADVISORY COMMITTEE ON THE SUPPLY AND TRAINING OF TEACHERS (ACSET). *Teacher Training and Special Educational Needs.* London: DES.

GREAT BRITAIN. DEPARTMENT OF EDUCATION AND SCIENCE (1985d). *Better Schools,* White Paper. London: HMSO.

GREAT BRITAIN. DEPARTMENT OF EDUCATION AND SCIENCE (1985b). *The First Year of TVEI.* HMI Report. London. DES.

GREAT BRITAIN. DEPARTMENT OF EDUCATION AND SCIENCE (1986a). *Working Together – Education and Training.* Cmnd 9823. London: HMSO.

GREAT BRITAIN. DEPARTMENT OF EDUCATION AND SCIENCE (1986b). *A Survey of the Lower Attaining Pupils Programme: The First Two Years.* Report on the HMI carried out between 1984 and 1985. London: DES.

GREAT BRITAIN. DEPARTMENT OF EDUCATION AND SCIENCE (1987a). FURTHER EDUCATION UNIT. *Coping to Confidence in Further Education.* London: DES.

GREAT BRITAIN. DEPARTMENT OF EDUCATION AND SCIENCE (1987b). *Quality in Schools.* London: HMSO.

GREAT BRITAIN. DEPARTMENT OF EDUCATION AND SCIENCE (1987). FURTHER EDUCATION UNIT. *Dilemma of Low Attainment.* London: DES.

HALLMARK, N. (1983). 'A support service to primary schools'. In: BOOTH, T. and POTTS, P. (Eds.) *Integrating Special Education.* Oxford, Blackwell.

HANNAM, C. (1975). *Parents and Mentally Handicapped Children.* Harmondsworth, Penguin.

HANSON, J. (1988). 'The Oxfordshire Skills Programme'. In: JONES, N. and SOUTHGATE, T. *Management and Special Needs: 11-19.* Beckenham: Croom Helm.

HARLAND, J. and WESTON, P. (1987). 'LAPP: Joseph's coat of many colours', *British Journal of Special Education,* 14,4.

HARGREAVES, . *Improving Secondary Schools* (The Hargreaves Report). London: ILEA.

HARRISON, M. (1981). 'Home start', *Early Childhood* 1,5.

HEART, S. (1986). 'Evaluating support teaching', *Gnosis,* 9,26-31.

HAYNES, C. (1986). 'The role of the speech therapist in a language school'. In: CRYSTAL, D. (Ed.) *Child Language, Teaching and Therapy,* Vol.1 London: Edward Arnold.

HEGARTY, S. and POCKLINGTON, K. (1981). *Educating Pupils with Special Educational Needs in Ordinary Schools.* Windsor: NFER-NELSON.

HEWISON, J. and TIZARD, J. (1980). 'Parental involvement and reading attainment', *British Journal of Educational Psychology* 50,209-215.

HEWISON, J. (1987). The Harringey Project, *Times Educationa Supplement,* 9.1.87.

HOCKLEY, L. (1985). 'On being a support teacher', *British Journal of Special Education* 12,1,27-29.

HODGSON, F. and TROTTER, A. (1988). 'In-service and special needs'. In: JONES, N.J. and SAYER, J., (Eds) *Management and the Psychology of Schooling.* Basingstoke: Falmer Press.

HOMANS, G.C. (1972). 'Social behaviour as exchange'. In: HOLLANDER, E.R. and HUNT, R.G. (Eds.) *Classic Contributions to Social Psychology.* Oxford: Oxford University Press.

HUMPHREYS, S. (1987). 'Participation in practice'. *Social Policy and Administration* 21,1,28-38.

IVIMEY, G. (1986). In: HEPTINSTALL, D., 'Will Warnock work?' *Speech Therapy in Practice* 2,3.

JACKSON, K. (1985). *The Art of Problem Solving.* Reading: Comino Foundation, Bulmershe College.

JONES, E. and BERRICK, S. (1985). 'Adopting a resource approach'. In: SMITH, C.J. (Ed.) *New Directions in Remedial Education.* Lewes: Falmer Press.

JONES, K. and REID, K. (1987). '6/86 and all that'. *Times Educational Supplement.* 6th November.

JONES, N. and SAYER, J. (1988). *Management and the Psychology of Schooling.* Basingstoke: Falmer Press.

KNOWLES, W. and MASIDLOVER, M. (1982). *Derbyshire Language Scheme.* Ripley: Derbyshire County Council.

LASKIER, M. (1985). 'The changing role of the remedial teacher', In: SMITH, C.J. (Ed.) *New Directions in Remedial Education.* Lewes: Falmer Press.

LAVERS, P., PICKUP, M. and THOMSON, M. (1986). 'Factors to consider in implementing an in-class support system within secondary schools', *Support for Learning* 1,3,32-35.

LEESON, P. (1988). 'Open and interactive learning: the LAPs Programme'. In: JONES, N. and SOUTHGATE, T. (Eds) *Management and Special Needs: 11-19.* Beckenham: Croom Helm.

Le PREVOST. 'Using the Makaton vocabulary in early language training with a Downs baby', *Mental Handicap* 11,28-29.

Le PROVOST, P. and DENNIS, J. (1985). *Communication, Speech and Language: How I Can Help.* Downs Children Association.

LEWIS, G. (1984). 'A supportive role at secondary level'. *Remedial Education* 19,1,7-12.

LEY, P. (1977). 'Psychological studies of doctor-patient communication'. In: RACHMAN, S., (Ed.) *Contributons to Medical Psychology.* Oxford: Pergamon.

LIPTON, H.L. and SVARSTAD, B. (1977). 'Sources of variation in clinical communication to parents about mental retardation', *American Journal of Mental Deficiency* 82,155-61.

LUTON, K. (1986). 'Learning by doing: the development of a whole-school approach', *Support for Learning* 1,4,22-30.

MANPOWER SERVICES COMMISSION (1984). *TVEI Review 1984.* London: MSC.

MASIDLOVER, M. (1980). Derbyshire Language Scheme. Education Office, Ripley, Derby.

MASON, F. (1986). The functioning of special school governing bodies. Unpublished diploma dissertation. London: West London Institute of Higher Education.

McBRIEN, J.A. and FOXEN, T.H. (1981). *The EDY In-service Course for Mental Handicap Practitioners*. Manchester: Manchester University Press.

McCONKEY, R. (1985). *Let's Play*. St. Michael's House, Upper Kilmacud Rd., Stillorgan, Co. Dublin.

McCONKEY, R. and GALLAGHER, F. (1984). *Let's Play Manual*. Ulster: Ulster Polytechnic and St. Michael's House.

McCONKEY, R. (1985). *Working with Parents: A Practical Guide for Teachers and Therapists*. London: Croom Helm.

McMURRAY, A. (1987). 'Comprehensive Schools and TVEI: a threat or a challenge?' In: BOOTH, T., POTTS, P. and SWANN, W. Eds) *Preventing Difficulties in Learning*. Oxford and Milton Keynes: Basil Blackwell and Open University Press.

MEHAN, H. (1983). 'The role of language and the language of role in institutional decision making', *Language Society* 12.

MITTLER, P. and MITTLER, H. (1982). Partnership with Parents. National Council for Special Education.

MITTLER, P. (1986). 'The new look in in-service training', *British Journal of Special Education*, 13,2.

MORGAN, R. (1988). 'Paired reading: its nature and current status'. In: JONES, N. (Ed.) *Curriculum and Integration 5-9*. (in preparation).

MOSES, D., HEGARTY, S. and JOWETT, S. (1987). *Local Authority Support Services*. Windsor: NFER-NELSON.

MOSES, D. and CROLL, P. (1987). 'Parents as partners or problems?' *Disability Handicap and Society* 2,1,75-83.

MOSES, D., HEGARTY, S. and JOWETT, S. (1987). 'Meeting special educational needs: support for the ordinary school', *Educational Research*. 29,2.

MUNN, P., HEWITT, G., MORRISON, A. and McINTYRE, D. (1982). *Accountability and Professionalism*. Stirling: University of Stirling Education Monograph.

MUNN, P. (1985). 'Accountability and parent-teacher communication', *British Educational Research Journal* 11,2,105-111.

NARE (1985). *Guidelines No.6: Teaching Roles for Special Educational Needs*. Stafford: NARE.

NEWCOMER, P.L. and HAMMILL, D.D. (1975). 'ITPA and academic achievement', *Reading Teacher*, 28,731-742.

PACT: (1984). *Home-school Reading Partnership in Hackney.* Hackney: Hackney Teachers' Centre.

PEARSON, L. and LINDSAY, G. (1987). *Special Needs in the Primary School: Identification and Intervention.* Windsor: NFER-NELSON.

PEDLER, M. and BOYDELL, T. (1985). *Managing Yourself.* London: Fontana.

PERRATON, H. (1987). 'Theories, generalisation and practice in distance education', *Open Learning*, 2,3, November. Harlow: Longman.

PETERS, R.S. (1972). 'Education as institution'. In: ARCHAMBAULT, R.D. *Philosophical Analysis and Education.* London: Routledge and Kegan Paul.

PLOWDEN, B. (1967). *Health and Services and the School Child.* London: HMSO.

POTTS, P. (1983). 'What difference would integration make to the professionals?' In: BOOTH, T. and POTTS, P. (Eds) *Integrating Special Education.* Oxford: Blackwell.

POTTS, P. (1987). *Project Guide: Really Useful Research – Finding Out For Yourselves.* Open University Course E806 Applied Studies in Learning Difficulties in Education. Milton Keynes: Open University Press.

PRINGLE, M.L.K. (1976). *The Needs of Children.* London: Hutchinson.

PRITCHARD, D.G. (1963). *Education and the Handicapped.* London: Routledge and Kegan Paul.

REVANS, R.W. (1980). *Action Learning.* London: Blond and Briggs.

ROAF, C. (1986). 'Whole school policy: principles into practice', *Forum for the Discussion of New Trends in Education* 29,1,20-22.

ROBSON, C. (1984). 'A modular in-service advanced qualification for teachers', *British Journal of In-service Education*, 11,1.

SAMPSON, O.C. (1975). 'A dream that is dying?' *Bulletin of the British Psychological Society*, 28,380-382.

SANDOW, S., STAFFORD, D. and STAFFORD, P. (1987). *An Agreed Understanding?* Windsor: NFER-NELSON.

SAYER, J. (1985). 'A whole-school approach to meeting all needs'. In: SAYER, J. and JONES, N. *Teacher Training and Special Educational Needs.* Beckenham: Croom Helm.

SAYER, J. (1985a). *What Future for Secondary Schools?* London: Falmer Press.

SAYER, J. and JONES, N. (1985). *Teacher Training and Special Educational Needs.* Beckenham: Croom Helm.

SEWELL, G. (1982). *Reshaping Remedial Education.* London: Croom Helm.

SHARRON, H. (1987). 'Changing children's minds', *Times Educational Supplement*, 22nd May.

SMITH, C. (1982). 'Helping colleagues cope: a consultation role for the remedial teacher', *Remedial Education* 17,2,75-79.

STENHOUSE, L. (1975). *An Introduction to Curriculum Research and Development.* London: Heinemann.

SUMMERFIELD. *Psychologists in the Education Service* (The Summerfield Report). London: HMSO.

SWANN, W. and BRIGGS, D. (1982). *A Special Curriculum ? Units 5/6.* Open University Course E241 Special Needs in Education. Milton Keynes: Open University Press.

SWANN, W. (1987). 'Is the integration of children with special needs happening? An analysis of recent statistics of pupils in special schools', *Oxford Review of Education, II.* 13-18.

TAYLOR, M. (1985). *Getting Things Done.* Further Education Unit. London: HMSO.

THOMAS, D. (1982). *The Experience of Handicap.* London: Methuen.

THOMAS, G. (1986). 'Integrating personnel in order to integrate children', *Support for Learning* 1,1,19-26.

THOMAS, G. and JACKSON, B. (1986). 'The whole school approach to integration', *British Journal of Special Education,* 13,1,27-29.

TIZARD, J. (1973). 'Maladjusted children and the Child Guidance Service', *London Educational Review,* 2,2,22-37.

TIZARD, B. and HUGHES, M. (1984). *Young Children Learning.* London: Fontana.

TOBIN, D. and PUMFREY, P. (1976). 'Some long-term effects of the remedial teaching of reading', *Educational Review* 29.

TOMLINSON, S. (1981). *Educational Subnormality: a study in decision making.* London: Routledge and Kegan Paul.

TOMLINSON, S. (1982). *A Sociology of Special Education.* London: Routledge and Kegan Paul.

TOMLINSON, S. (1985). 'The expansion of special education', *Oxford Review of Education* 11,2,157-165.

TRENAMAN, J. (1967). *Communication and Comprehension.* Harlow: Longman.

VISSER, J. (1986). 'Support; a description of the work of the SEN professional', *Support for Learning* 1,4,5-9.

WAKEFIELD, A. (1985). 'New approaches to assessment: some issues of ownership and control', *Secondary Headteachers Association Review,* LXXIX, 247, December.

WALDON, G. *The Asocial Lesson.* Centre for Educating Young Handicapped Children at Home. Didsbury: Manchester.

WALDON, G. (1983). 'Understanding Understanding.' Vol. 2. KOINE.

WARNOCK, M. (1978). *Special Educational Needs. Report of the Committee of Enquiry into the Education of Handicapped Children and Young People.* (The Warnock Report). London: HMSO.

WATERLAND, E. (1985). *Read With Me: An apprenticeship approach to reading*. Stroud: Thimble Press.

WATKINS, P. (1986). *Modular Approaches to the Secondary Curriculum*. London: Longman.

WEATHERLEY, R. (1979). *Reforming Special Education: Policy Implementation from State Level to Street Level*. Cambridge, Mass., and London: MIT Press.

WEBSTER, A. and McCONNELL, C. (1987). *Children with Speech and Language Difficulties*. London: Cassell.

WEDELL, K., WELTON, J., EVANS J. and GOACHER, B. (1987). *The 1981 Education Act: Policy and Provision for Special Educational Needs*. London: Department of Education and Science.

WELLS, G. (1984). *Language Development in the Pre-school Years*. Cambridge: Cambridge University Press.

WELLS, C.G. (1987). *The Meaning Makers*. Cambridge: Cambridge University Press.

WELTON, J. and EVANS, J. (1986). 'The development and implementation of special education policy: where did the 1981 Act fit in?', *Public Administration* Vol. 64 Summer pp.209-227.

WIDLAKE, P. (1983). *How to Reach the Hard to Teach*. Milton Keynes: Open University Press.

WIDLAKE, P. (1986). *Reducing Educational Disadvantage*. Milton Keynes: Open University Press.

YOUNG, I. (1987). East Oxfordshire special needs team: report on the primary schools questionnaire. Unpublished dissertation, Oxford Polytechnic.